ENEMY OF INJUSTICE

Andrew with Philip Snowdon at Scarborough 1920

ENEMY OF INJUSTICE

The Life of Andrew MacLaren

Member of Parliament

Malcolm Hill

OTHILA PRESS
1999

OTHILA PRESS

58a Abingdon Road
London W8

First published 1999

Second edition

ISBN 1 901647 19 6

Andrew's life was dedicated to the struggle for natural birthrights

Contents

	List of illustrations	ix
	Acknowledgements	x
	Foreword	xi
	Introduction	xiii
1	Early Influences	1
2	Cause of Poverty	8
3	Radical Apprenticeship	19
4	Constitutional Débâcle	27
5	First World War	39
6	Candidate for Parliament	52
7	Member of Parliament	66
8	Member for Burslem	81
9	Ducal and Shavian Interludes	99
10	Protection Safeguarded	121
11	Land Question	132
12	Coalition and Confusion	143
13	Second World War	159
14	Retirement	175
15	Conclusion	186
	Index	189

Illustrations

Andrew and Philip Snowden   *Frontispiece*

Andrew with Stanley Baldwin   *Between pp. 32–3*
Andrew with Bernard Shaw
Andrew at a gathering in the Potteries
Andrew on his way to Rio de Janeiro in 1929
Andrew's drawing of Neville Chamberlain after Munich

Who made the earth?   *Between pp. 64–5*
Title Deeds
Rates
Disarmament Conference
Two Prime Ministers
Churchill swimming

Acknowledgements

My gratitude is extended to the executors of Andrew MacLaren's Literary Estate. It is also due to Harry Dunbar, Paul Turner, Geoffrey Lee and Christopher Scarfe for pulling the manuscript into shape.

Foreword

I met Andrew MacLaren in the summer of 1958, six months after my arrival in London from Hong Kong. He was in his mid-seventies and I only twenty-four. For the next seventeen years until his death in 1975 our relationship was one of friendship. Despite the difference of half a century in our ages, he always treated me as an equal with courtesy and respect. He was the principal influence in my life and this was affected without setting himself up as my teacher: his example was sufficient and, indeed, unusual.

Andrew owed his education to Nature. His attitude to everything was universal. He learned his basic skills without the advantage of formal schooling. That is more difficult and also more intelligent than it seems, for man is subject to many influences of a worldly nature and the pull to conform is very strong. Andrew became a cultured man. In music he found, from his initiation as a choir-boy in his father's choir, most evidence of the soulfulness and the most sublime expression of man's nature. He painted and had a great interest in the work of others and for a time was a noted cartoonist for several publications. But music remained the most ineffable art for him.

Andrew's humour was robust. I remember when he and I attended a concert at the Albert Hall, London, at the invitation of Sir Malcolm Sargent. We were seated directly behind the conductor's rostrum. At the interval Andrew motioned me to leave, because he complained that Sir Malcolm 'was showing off' at the expense of the music. I enjoyed with him a close friendship with Jennifer Vyvian, the soprano.

Andrew believed that the progress of civilisation gave rise to societies which contained the diversity and creativity of individuals, interwoven, as it were, into the fabric of society. Yet he was adamant that in this condition the individual does not need to sacrifice his birthright: to enjoy his right to the natural elements of air, sunshine, water and land. As an independent Labour Member of Parliament, he worked tirelessly for the causes which reflected his political conviction.

He delighted in passing on ideas to young people; recognising the rising humanity and open-mindedness of the new generation. He lamented the lack of education in youth in what might be called political wisdom. He continued to give talks in London until five days before he died, aged ninety-two.

I learned from him the need for independence, which seemed to him an essential prerequisite of the dignity of man. He lived without accepting honours or public remuneration because he refused to accept 'the system of society'. Always his own integrity was his most precious jewel. Becoming independent meant a great deal to me in my commercial life. Indeed, earning a living has been an enjoyment, rather than a servitude.

I became a great friend of Moira Forsyth who was Andrew's companion in later life. In gratitude for their friendship I named my son, Andrew, and my daughter, Moira.

In this biography I commend the line taken by the author between the private life of Andrew, which belonged to him alone, and his thinking as a man in public life. History, asserted Andrew, should be a record of the public domain; speculations about private life were, he thought, trivial.

I hope reading about a man, whom I was honoured to call a friend, will impart to the readers a little of the richness which I gained from Andrew MacLaren.

Holland Kwok
London 1999

Introduction

Britain is a democratic nation but its people are not in control of their lives. Posterity may admire the British for their skill and courage in creating a democratic framework for society. During modern history they wrested power from tyrants and placed it in their own hands. The purpose, it might be reasonably presumed, was to create a just society in which the rights of the weak individual ranked with those of the strong. The hardware of secret and regular elections, freedom of speech, open trial and other constitutional institutions of democracy have been secured over the last three centuries. But the software of the people's political thinking has not been developed. Society is riven by an unjust distribution of wealth which bestows on a few individuals riches and poverty on the masses.

Britain has the potential for justice, freedom and prosperity but it lacks the fight and the will to bring these about. Posterity will surely conclude that the British assembled the institutions to destroy injustice in the distribution of wealth and yet were too timid to employ them. They enjoy civil liberties after a long fight over three centuries, but of economic liberty they remain ignorant. Free men have a right to both and, yet, they put up with poverty, inflation and unemployment as though they were the natural order of society.

This is a book about a British political thinker who sought to make men and women aware of the economic condition of society. He believed that freedom was the principal endeavour and the creation of a free society was a worthy ideal of man.

After Andrew MacLaren served in local government in Stoke on Trent and the House of Commons during the 1920s and 30s he lectured in London in the 1960s. In his late eighties he still spoke with undiminished passion and clarity. His humour was generous and his understanding of society's economic condition was precise. He had an independent mind which moved from history, art and spiritual values to economic and political commentary, with such ease that he made it seem these subjects were each part of man's freedom. He did not distinguish between spiritual freedom, civil or economic freedom: freedom needed no categorisation or definition. It was, to him, the birthright of man.

In appearance he was striking. His eyes were blue and clear. His overall demeanour was of alertness. His hair was half black and half white and his jaw jutted fearlessly forward, lending his countenance an unmistakable authority. His voice was vigorous and his laughter infectious when under control, but it broke into an unrestrained chuckle of delight when frequently it was not. His voice was notable for the unrestrained trace of his native Scottish accent.

He had no appetite for public office. To briefly hold an office of State and then to leave the stage with an honour was nothing to his mind, when compared with upholding the magnificence of Nature, who was the mother of man. His devotion to justice gave intellectual integrity a fresh meaning. Not once over a period of five years before his death did he utter a sentiment at variance with his principles.

The most abiding impression of Andrew was of a man who was incapable of lying. Certainly not out of any superior moral sense, but simply because only truth interested him. He believed firmly in Nature. She provided a rich planet with every resource of which man had need. But man has contemptuously set aside this gift and disfigured it with war, poverty, the petty tyrannies of ignorance, the poisons of technology, the blindness induced by expertise and the conceits of man. He spoke for no particular class of men but for the individual; class meant nothing to him.

In his mind he saw the individual as a free being, free to earn what he produced, free to live in good, beautiful, housing, think noble thoughts, eat nourishing food and educate himself and his family to appreciate artistic and creative works of man. Nature, he believed, was an unconditional benefactor of mankind. But whenever he turned to consider man in society, his dream was shattered by reality. Fresh horrors of man's

INTRODUCTION

inhumanity were reported daily by the media. Often man's nobility was destroyed by conceit, selfishness and pettiness. He felt that tragedy and comedy were often different faces of the same coin.

There was no trace of sentimentality in Andrew. From one who revered the natural order, one would not have expected to find any within him. Nor was there any weary wisdom which he might have accumulated during a long life. He was alert, quick minded and his humour was always refreshing.

Although he had a penetrating mind and a keen mental discipline, he was a warm-hearted friend. He was drawn to honest characters and he had an artist's sympathy and eye for the human predicament.

To hear Andrew talking about the way the British electorate allowed their birthright to be trampled by politicians and their parties immediately awakened a deep interest in the civil and economic rights of man. Politics and parliament are generally tedious and dull, because neither are often concerned with true principles of political thought. For the most part they are preoccupied with superficiality and sentimentality. Andrew felt that education of youth was seriously deficient in making no provision for the teaching of political thought without regard to party politics. For at a certain age, between about 16 and 25, the natural impulse in every heart is to be just and humane. Instead young people are reared, after their ideals have perished along with their youth, with the foolery poured forth by political parties. Andrew distrusted government when the people had no understanding of political thought and particularly the control of taxation and education. He provoked thought, he excited minds, he championed justice, democracy, prosperity and humanity. His role in the history of political thought in a tradition which has endured from the eighteenth century will be remembered in this account of his life. He will become a friend of those who will fight for heaven to be introduced on earth.

1

Early Influences

Andrew MacLaren was born on 28 May 1883, the son of the choirmaster at St. Francis' Church in Glasgow. Probably the strongest influence during his formative years was his Irish grandmother, who inspired him by her fearless thinking and speaking. 'I remember,' he once recalled, 'that my grandmother, who was very Irish, used to remind me when I went to Mass on Sunday morning that God made the land for the people, "but," she said, "it is not God who comes round for the rent on Monday morning." '[1] He also remembered her fulminating over the refrain that Britannia ruled the waves. 'Waves!' she snorted, 'it is land that we need, not waves.' And her saying: 'In Ireland we have shot more landlords than any country on God's earth, but in England they put them in castles and call them gentlemen.' These declarations reverberated throughout MacLaren's life.

When his grandmother sent him to bed, she instilled in him the dread that, if he was naughty, Lord Leitrim would emerge from under his bed. To guard against such a fearsome event, MacLaren wore a miraculous medallion around his neck and hung an oleograph of Pope Leo XII giving a benediction above his bed. At the age of seven he lost his grandmother and felt that he had no friend alive. When he was ninety years old MacLaren occasionally enacted the scene of himself as a child at her knee. With a few gestures he contrasted the admiration of youth with the powerful rhetoric of an independent spirit.

In later life he seldom referred to his family life in Glasgow

---

[1] Hansard, col. 2047; 14:12:38.

and was insistent that no one should research this period of his life because he regarded childhood as a private matter. The little that is known of his childhood is drawn from his public sources.

His family were poor. As he recalled:

> My own experience was too bitter to ever forget it. I had a mother who tried to rear a family, but met with disaster. There is nothing more terrible than when poverty strikes a house and those who are in it know there is a better life than the one they are living. I shall never forget when the demand for rates were knocking at our door. We could have managed to pay the high rental, but when the rates came on top of it, it plunged our household into absolute misery.[1]

The Glasgow Corporation had trouble with a neighbour who awaited the arrival of the dreaded rating demand armed only with her pride and a pair of bellows, with which the demand was blown back out beneath the door. How, she demanded of the Corporation, could rates be imposed on such a draughty house? MacLaren's family moved to south Glasgow where he attended St. Francis' School. The adjoining church had been designed by Pugin and its ample proportions made a deep impression on him. He became interested in the history of Assisi and the frescoes of Giotto. Many a Saturday he lingered in the aisle of the church and would build a picture in his mind of how it had looked in its pre-Reformation state. He was indignant that this relic of medieval beauty should have fallen into the hands of austere Presbyterians. The world of the church was rich in art and music, far removed from the general poverty around; the squalor of the notorious slums in the Gorbals, the drunkenness, the broken bottles and broken lives, the prostitution and the degradation of the human spirit. At home the conversation was of politics – Parnell, Gladstone, Irish Home Rule – and religion – Newman and Manning. His father was a passionate admirer of Mozart, Haydn, Beethoven and Palestrina.

MacLaren's childhood formed the inspiration for many of his later public talks to women on the significance of their natural

---

[1] Ibid., col. 1877; 23:6:42.

task of rearing children physically, mentally and spiritually. He readily acknowledged that the power of the hand that rocked the cradle also fashioned the destinies of nations. Later, as a father himself, he told the House of Commons:

> The home is the place where the woman has to bring forth her children and the place in which the little children touch the knee and ask the first question and receive the first answer. It is the home, as I said before, that marks the beginning of the spiritual development of the race.[1]

At school MacLaren was a rebel. He was not interested in sport and considered the study of dead languages and the dismal history of battles and other struggles for power a waste of time. His education seemed dominated by the voluminous evidence of man's inability to live peaceably in society and the young MacLaren was concerned to know the causes, rather than the consequences, of man's sad condition.

From an early age MacLaren displayed a talent for drawing. Once, during an examination, he drew his first caricature. It was of Joseph Chamberlain, the English politician, blowing bubbles into the air. The invigilator caught him but although it lay in his power to punish the artist he decided, on seeing the drawing, to encourage this talent and asked MacLaren to do another one immediately. He then drew another caricature of Chamberlain posting up fiscal reform bills.

At the age of ten MacLaren left school to help maintain his father's considerable family. He began work at 3s 6d per week in a tailoring firm, attending drawing classes in the evening. But after three years, as an escape from the ugliness of poverty and the harsh realities of commerce, he sought to join the Benedictine order.

A monastery had opened at Fort Augustus on the southern tip of Loch Ness. A number of monks went regularly to Glasgow. MacLaren became friendly with a Brother Celeste and was allowed to join a week's retreat at the monastery, at the end of which the Abbot met him. He rejected MacLaren's request to join the monastery, insisting that he first discuss it with his

---

[1] Ibid., col. 301; 15:3:44.

parents. The Abbot noted his talent for public speaking and suggested that he was not suited to follow the life of a recluse.

MacLaren's deep affection for the monks is reflected in some correspondence between them in the years 1899 to 1903. These tender, warm-hearted letters from the fraternity reflect the great fondness and love they had for MacLaren, referring to him as both their friend and spiritual child. Brother Celeste also observed MacLaren's talent for speaking but counselled him to be aware that this talent was God-given. He would always speak well, the monk affirmed, but if he spoke on his own behalf he would impart only information, rather than understanding. Throughout his life MacLaren remembered Brother Celeste's advice. He always sought to communicate with the soul of an audience, aiming directly at their sense of reason and justice.

His father thought MacLaren should equip himself with worldly knowledge and dismissed the idea of his becoming a monk. He compelled MacLaren, at the age of fourteen, to become an apprentice engineer. MacLaren, however, was determined to study at the Glasgow School of Art and he joined its evening class in life drawing while continuing his general studies at evening classes at the Technical College. As a receipt shows the fee was £1 per term. During the lunch hour in the engineer's shop MacLaren used to read the newspapers to the engineers and fellow apprentices, often provoking debates on a variety of subjects. These debates were conducted according to strict rules and MacLaren often observed that Scotsmen learnt a more precise use of language than the English. Sometimes the Irish engineers would recite long passages of Shakespeare, Burns or Shelley.

Not surprisingly, MacLaren felt the strain of working daily from 6.00 am to 10.00 pm and was grateful to his colleagues who lowered their voices in order to allow him some rest, for they knew he 'went to collidge (sic) in the evening.'

On the tram MacLaren would read the historical works of either Gibbon or Buckle. He was always struck by the sight of other men gazing avidly at pages on horse racing and football.

MacLaren remembered fitting diamond cutters to coal diggers and observing that such a technological innovation, while increasing the output of coal, did not similarly increase miners' wages. Throughout his life, he was touched by the simple piety of mining communities and by the way they turned to religion and prayer at times of distress.

After his father's death, the standard of the St. Francis' Church choir deteriorated. Although he was growing less committed to the Church, MacLaren stepped in to conduct them and the choir began to regain some of its former quality. When he was conducting he could not help observing the beauty of the choristers. As he brought the baton down he noticed that they were all concentrating on the music rather than on themselves. Then, for a moment, they seemed like angels. However, the older members began to whisper about his lack of religious faith and, in consequence, MacLaren resigned his position and left the Church.

He loved music and particularly Mozart, whom he regarded as a supreme artist, though he later developed a strong feeling for Elgar. In October 1900, the Birmingham premier of Elgar's oratorio, *The Dream of Gerontius*, set to words by Cardinal Newman, was a disappointment. It was, however, acclaimed in two later productions in Dusseldorf where it was said there that England, 'the land without music', had found a composer of international status. Elgar was called back twenty times at the end of the first part. After a later performance, MacLaren remembered being thrilled at the opportunity to offer his umbrella to the composer as he left the hall.

MacLaren was forbidden by his parents from cutting through the Gorbals on his way to work so he used to travel round them by tram. One night, however, he had to take a short-cut through them to save time. He went past a second-hand book shop advertising a rather expensive two volume edition of a translation of Marx's *Das Kapital*. He returned later to browse through them and fell into conversation with the Jewish bookseller. He offered to let MacLaren borrow a volume at a time on condition that he explain their contents to him. Though Marx's ideas proved to be beyond MacLaren's comprehension, the bookseller took to him and invited him to a family gathering. From MacLaren's recollection, a listener could sense the 'smell' of the evening. The air was heavy with incense, the prayers were intense and sincere, the welcome to him was warm. After the meal the bookseller introduced him to the *Guide to the Perplexed* by Maimonides, a Jewish philosopher of the twelfth century.

At seventeen MacLaren qualified as an engineer though he still hoped to become a monk; to return to the world of gothic cloisters and chant *Solemne*. However, there was the need to look after his family which had been plunged into dire poverty following his father's death. He, therefore, remained an engineer, turning to Newman's *Apologia* and his university lectures for spiritual inspiration.

Though economic needs drove him back to the noise and clatter of cogwheels, chisels and files, his studies proceeded with Karl Marx and his sense of beauty remained undimmed. By twenty-one, his cherished religious and political faiths were further undermined by his reading. Gibbon's *Decline and Fall* opened new dimensions of thought. This work led on to Dr. Samuel Dell's *Roman Society*. His spiritual faith was also challenged by Locke, Hume and the French *encyclopédistes*.

When he was eighteen or so he went on a cycling tour of Ireland. One night he was delighted to stop wearily at a lighted house where he was warmly welcomed. He enquired on arrival why the owner kept an ugly looking blunderbuss hanging above the chimney. The owner replied that he kept the weapon to pay the rent. MacLaren began to feel at home in such a fearlessly practical country.

At the Glasgow School of Art, he studied the techniques of the great painters, particularly Rembrandt and Velasquez, until he had acquired a foundation for drawing and oil painting. He observed particularly how the great artists were able to exercise their power of selection in order to raise some everyday scene or emotion to a higher level of experience.

A motive behind MacLaren's reading of history was to learn more about human society and the causes of poverty. Only Marx seemed to shed light on this predicament and although *Das Kapital* seemed abstruse and dry MacLaren persisted in order to learn the message which he believed Marx had to offer him.

At that time religious bigotry was ever present, entering every area of life; nowhere so obtrusively as the work place. Employers would invariably take on Protestants only and notices advertising vacancies often stated that 'Irish need not apply'. Though these practices were defended as preserving the sanctity of religions, MacLaren considered them to be the main features of an insecure society. In themselves they were social poisons. He often remembered the epigram which an Irishman had chalked up on derelict walls. 'You are not what you think you are. If you are not what you think you are, then, in the name of God, what are you?'

MacLaren's love of debate drew him into the political life of Glasgow. He attended many meetings as a speaker or participant, sometimes contriving with other hot-heads to undermine a platform with a series of prepared questions. Many a visiting politician did not return in a hurry to Glasgow. It was after all the second city of the Empire and it might have been supposed to include its fair share of imperial zealots.

One evening in 1908 MacLaren spoke in a debate on education. After the meeting John Paul and his brother came forward to congratulate him on his speech. They said how much they had admired the manner of its delivery, while expressing their reservation about its want of political understanding. MacLaren's guardian angel must have been present because he accepted their criticism and readily borrowed a book which they offered to him. It is difficult for those who knew him later ever to imagine MacLaren accepting such a direct criticism; for the critic, not only was this like putting his head into a lion's mouth, but far more reckless since it was certain to be bitten off.

The book was Henry George's *Progress and Poverty* and, upon reading it, MacLaren felt a bringing together of his spiritual and artistic quests. For, while other books merely commented on history, lacking any real insight into the cause of things, this one clearly identified the cause of poverty in society.

2

The Cause of Poverty

By the time he read a few chapters of *Progress and Poverty* MacLaren realised he was on the path leading directly towards the solution of a problem which had haunted him for so long. The book, he felt, contrasted the handiwork of Nature, which was perfect and munificent, with the imperfections of Man. George had a clear vision of the cause of poverty; he understood that the ills of the world were due to the ignorance of man. If men failed to base their society on the model of Nature they would fall into an ever deepening whirlpool of confusion and disaster. The natural order of peace and prosperity would be replaced by human fear and misery.

MacLaren derived great inspiration from the principles embraced by George but he never became a sectarian follower of him. He believed that no man could claim such ideas as his own; ideas were common property, like fresh air, and larger than any particular mind. However, it is worth pausing to consider the philosophy and life of George in order to explain the foundation of MacLaren's political thinking.

Henry George had lived much of his adult life in California. He worked on several newspapers, first as printer and later as an editor. Throughout his life he was dogged by extreme poverty. For though the American dream is associated invariably with prosperity, the experience for the mass of the population was often the reverse. In the mid-1860s depression was relieved temporarily by the discovery of gold and then by the development of the railroad system. But the experience of depression was otherwise bleak.

The lowest point to which George sank was after his wife had

THE CAUSE OF POVERTY

been delivered of her second child. He had no work and no money and had to beg for food. As he approached the first well-dressed stranger he saw in the street, George, normally a lawful man, decided to rob him if he was unwilling to help. Fortunately, the man took pity on him and gave him five dollars.

For a decade George puzzled over the richness of man's potential – how he could satisfy his every need – and yet how the mass of society suffered what he termed 'the hell of poverty'. The answer to this riddle of human existence came to him at first gradually and then in two moments of inspiration. This he described in his book *Progress and Poverty* which was published in 1879.

MacLaren was struck by George's drawing aside the veil on questions long supposed to have been settled in European thought. In narrating what was actually occurring during the colonisation of the savannah in the American West, George described how the first settler in a community could pitch his tent anywhere since as far as the eye could see there was no human habitation. But man is gregarious by nature and the second settler tended to choose a site adjacent to the first settler. Gradually, the best land attracted an owner and later settlers were left with the choice of land of lower quality. In time, artisans and professionals gathered and a community began to form. Land came to have an ever greater value in relation to the increasing demand for its use.

Certain public works – like road maintenance and lighting, bridges, public utilities, police, fire forces and railways – needed to be provided, but whose expenses were beyond the means of most individuals. Yet the value of land, which had been steadily rising with the arrival of new settlers, provided a natural fund at the disposal of the community. Furthermore, the provision of these essential services further increased the value of land.

It was established in America, as in Europe, that land could lawfully be the private property of an individual. But the greater number had arrived too late to find a piece of unoccupied land and they depended, therefore, on their labour, which they were obliged to offer to the landed. The level of wages being set by the competition among the landless seeking work.

George distinguished two spheres of wealth; private and

public. Labour, whether performed by an individual or private collection of individuals, created private wealth. But a community created public wealth which rightly belonged to all its members in equal degree. No one, from a baby in a pram to a monarch on a throne, had a greater claim than any other upon this communally created wealth since it arose from the growth and existence of a community.

MacLaren could see that the underlying truth of George's observation of a growing society was of universal application and that the facts which George exposed were the same everywhere. In Scotland, for example, the value of a building was considered quite apart from the value of the land on which it stood. MacLaren quickly grasped this distinction between buildings made by man and land which was the gift of Nature to all men in common.

MacLaren came to see land as a natural resource just like fresh air, sunshine and water; they were essential elements of life. He understood that, in the natural order, land value could never be claimed as private property. For property in anything can only be acquired in one of three ways. Labour can acquire property. Thus property in, say, a piece of furniture, rests in the first place with its maker. The property of the maker can be passed by gift or purchase. Thus, a house can be passed down the generations by gift or by purchase without ever acquiring the merest vestige of public property. A free society would hold private property inviolate in its possession, at least in times of peace. There are no true grounds for private property to be taxed.

However, no individual has created land value. For land does not become valuable until two people want the same piece. Land value is a measurement of the strength of demand for its use. No one wants to live in the Sahara Desert and so its land has no value. Property in land value remains with the community who created it. It was upon this prime distinction in property that George was most illuminating and his thinking formed the Pole Star in MacLaren's political compass. By permitting public wealth to fructify in private pockets, governments were forced to tax the labour and production of individuals.

Though landowners protested that they had acquired property in land value by inheritance or gift according to human law,

Nature gave land value to the community and not to individuals. Humans possess free-will to devise whatever human laws they wish, but even the entire assemblage of human majesty on earth, even the most venerable tradition, cannot declare Nature invalid. The law of gravity cannot be outlawed though it can, of course, be ignored. In effect, landowners do just that. But if human law does not observe the laws of Nature, it will create disorder.

Forgetting the original process by which a landowner came into possession of the value of land, the question can be considered reasonably. Landowners can base their title on no more substantial ground than upon the consent of their fellow men to their possession. Realising that their title to land rests on no weightier consideration, the landowning interests have ensured that any questioning of their title has been kept out of political or public debate. The matter has been suppressed as unthinkable.

George had described the cause of poverty: the land belonged to the few rich and powerful and the masses were landless and poor. The landowning interests controlled society by exerting influence over economic thought and debate, and through education.

He also pointed to the solution: that the community recover the land value which it created through taxation. The justice of such a move cannot be refuted. For if an individual or a community wishes to have exclusive possession of land on which to live or work, it is surely just that they repay to their fellow men the value which the latter have created and agreed to forgo.

While writing *Progress and Poverty*, which must have seemed like walking a lone road, George took much encouragement from a renowned contemporary English thinker, Herbert Spencer. His works were well known in America and, when writing about the possession of land, he wrote in the most unambiguous terms as this passage from his book, *Social Statics*, shows.

> Equity does not permit property in land. The assumption that land can be held as property involves that the whole

globe may become the private domain of a part of its inhabitants and that the rest of the population are trespassers thereon. It can never be pretended that the existing titles to such property, are legitimate. Should anyone think so let him look at the Chronicles. Violence, fraud, the prerogative of force, the claims of superior cunning – these are the sources to which those titles may be traced. The original deeds were written with the sword rather than with the pen; not lawyers but soldiers were the conveyancers, blows the current coins given in payment; and for the seals, blood used in preference to wax. Could valid claims be thus constituted?[1]

Later he was even more specific when he wrote: 'Either men have a right to make the soil private property, or they have not. There is no medium. We must choose one of the two positions. There can be no half opinions. In the nature of things the fact must be one way or the other.'[2] Yet Spencer later repudiated the ideas contained in *Social Statics* and George found himself alone once more.

It is widely held that human government can devise whatever tax it wishes and almost everything that moves in society is taxed as a result. And although it is argued that taxes fall chiefly on the rich, the reality is that the rich become richer under such taxation while the poor remain poor. For taxation, both direct and indirect, passes on into the price of commodities and so is paid proportionately more heavily by the poor. While government can devise taxation after its whim, it cannot prevent the consequences of unjust taxation from occurring.

The skill in raising taxes was described in the seventeenth century as the art of plucking as many feathers from a fowl without making it squawk. In the twentieth century it has come to consist of giving the appearance that the tax is being paid by the rich when, in reality, it is borne by the poor.

MacLaren knew from his study of history that, in England, poverty had remained unreformed and so had been flourishing since the middle of the sixteenth century. The various efforts to

---
[1] Spencer, H., *Social Statics*, Ch.9.
[2] *Land Values*, 12:1:04.

mitigate it, like the Poor Law and the Settlement Acts, which confined individuals to their parishes, had failed utterly to stem its outbreak or interrupt its persistence. George had diagnosed a problem unfolding as the empty American West was filling with immigrants. Yet MacLaren saw that the problem existed in Britain in a society in which land was fully enclosed.

By 1850 the study of economics was running on lines drawn by Adam Smith, Ricardo and John Stuart Mill. Though it was widely accepted that they were the true founders of economic thinking none of them had seriously considered the land question. Smith daintily trod round both it and the whole question of taxation in order to avoid upsetting vested interests while Ricardo dwelt exclusively on agricultural land. Mill had simply avoided any full discussion of the question in his writing at all. In Britain they had established a false orthodoxy in economic thought and pretended that it was the orthodoxy of economic history. MacLaren could see only that their reasoning was faulty; he believed that the profundity of ideas depended on their simplicity. Not until the last month of his life did he learn that, before Smith, the French statesman, Turgot, had formulated the study of economics around the principle advocated – more fully after the Industrial Revolution – by George: that the value of land afforded the one species of public property which should be recovered for the benefit of society through taxation.

It is a wonder that adults should enter public life with little or no idea of either the history or the principles of free trade. It is an established fact that protection is always defective in its application and incalculably destructive of prosperity and peace. The lack of economic knowledge on free trade may be likened to a student assuming that the world is flat; to graduate in that pitiful state of ignorance is sad. Yet politicians are ever looking for additional *raison d'être*; political control of trade, of money and economies offers the semblance of reality to their public existence. George wrote about the virtues of free trade – that is, trade between people of different nations, in the market place of the entire globe, without any political interference. He regarded free trade as the natural complement to free land. Conversely, he regarded protectionism – the denial of free trade – an adjunct to the private appropriation of land value. Free trade is a simple concept to understand. George made it intelligible to a child in his second book, *Protection or Free Trade*, where the full argument is well and comprehensively presented.

While writing this book George observed the scene in a field outside his study window:

> a great bull is tethered by a ring in his nose. Grazing round and round, he has wound his rope about the stake until now he stands a close prisoner, tantalised by rich grass he cannot reach, unable even to toss his head to rid him of the flies that cluster on his shoulders. Now and again he struggles vainly, and then, after pitiful bellowing, relapses into silent misery. This bull, a very type of massive strength, who, because he has not wit enough to see how he might be free, suffers want in sight in plenty, and is helplessly played upon by weaker creatures, seems to me no unfit emblem for the working masses.

In 1881, two years before MacLaren's birth, George visited the British Isles. Ireland was suffering from depressed agricultural prices and there was considerable resentment of English rule. Tenant farmers were regularly evicted by landlords, often by English absentee landlords. The English parliament had passed a new Land Act in 1881 protecting the tenure of tenants, fixing their rents and creating a proprietorial title in improvements they might effect. During the resulting unrest, Charles Parnell, the political leader of the Irish in the House of Commons, was jailed and from prison declared a policy of withholding rent payments until the British government restored full constitutional rights to the Irish people and ended the state of terror. During his visit to Ireland, George met Bishop Nulty, whose thinking resembled his own. Nulty had written: 'The system of land tenure in Ireland had created a human existence which in strict truth and justice can be characterised as the twin sister of slavery.'[1] George was clearly shocked by what he saw in Ireland and declared the British government 'the

---
[1] Barker, C., *Henry George*, p. 350.

most damnable government that exists outside Russia.'[1] Though he did not support the campaign to withhold rent, George argued it should be paid to the State: a thesis he argued in another book, *The Irish Land Question*, and in several letters to the press. For his pains, he was arrested twice on suspicion of criminal activity.

He also made fleeting visits to London where he met, and profoundly influenced, George Bernard Shaw. Shaw immediately recognised that George was an American 'because, he pronounced "necessarily" – a favourite word of his – with the accent on the third syllable instead of the first; because he was deliberately and intentionally oratorical, which is not customary among such shy people like the English; because he spoke of Liberty, Justice, Truth, Natural Law and other strange eighteenth century superstitions; and because he explained with great simplicity and sincerity the views of the Creator who had gone completely out of fashion in London in the previous decade and had not been heard of since. I noticed also that he was a born orator, and that he had small plump and pretty hands . . . The result of my hearing the speech, and buying from one of the stewards of the meeting a copy of *Progress and Poverty* for sixpence [Heaven only knows where I got that sixpence] was that I plunged into a course of economic study, and at a very early stage became a socialist and spoke from that very platform on the same subject, and from hundreds of others as well . . . When thus swept into the great Socialist revival of 1883, I found that five-sixths of those who were swept in with me had been converted by Henry George.'[2]

Persuaded that the sale of *Progress and Poverty* in Britain would advance George's reputation in America, Shaw personally subsidised[3] a low-cost edition, of which half a million copies had been sold throughout Britain before 1884. The Liberals, however, disliked his confiscation of land value without provision for compensation, a proposition which, to George, was the same as the demands of compensation for the slave

---

[1] Ibid., p. 347.
[2] Ibid., p. 376.
[3] Ibid., p. 375.

owners. As George was advocating the collection of what he had shown to be communal, rather than individual, property, there was no basis for compensation.

George once spoke at Oxford University. After his speech Alfred Marshall, then a lecturer at Balliol and later the renowned economist, observed that the speaker did not understand an author whom he had criticised in his work. However, he would not censure George on this score since it was clear that he was not properly trained. Such condescension, as MacLaren often pointed out, has often marked university learning. It matters not, apparently, that the language of academic economists is so far above the understanding of ordinary people that it has become an irrelevant discipline, bereft of simple principles, sustained by meaningless statistics and advanced by theoretical and subjective notions. Indeed vested interests have manipulated economists to their own advantage; the more incomprehensible economics becomes, the less dangerous its tenets are to those who have most to fear from its study.

Count Leo Tolstoy became a convert to the ideas formulated by George and wrote several essays – *A Great Iniquity, The Slavery of Our Times, Resurrection* and *The Root of the Evil* – on the land question. He wrote to George suggesting a meeting in Russia. But George, probably unaware of Tolstoy's growing reputation, allowed the correspondence to lapse. Years later Tolstoy greeted George's son with the words: 'Your father was my friend.' In an interview with the *Pall Mall Gazette* he said: 'In thirty years time private property in land will be as much a thing of the past as is now serfdom. England, America and Russia will be the first to solve the problem ... Henry George had formulated the next article in the programme of the progressive Liberals of the world.'[1]

In a passage, which closely resembles MacLaren's thinking, Tolstoy wrote:

> Yet the ownership of land ... has not the least justification, because land, like water, air, or the rays of the sun, is an indispensable condition of every man's life ... therefore it

---
[1] George, H. jnr, *The Life of Henry George*, p. 514.

cannot be the exclusive property of one person. If land, and not water, air, or solar rays, has become the object of property, it is not because land is not just as indispensable a condition of every man's existence, which cannot therefore be appropriated, but because it is not possible to deprive men of water, or air, or the sun, whereas it is possible to deprive them of land. Landed property was established by violence . . . and in spite of all the attempts to transform it into a right, it has still remained nothing but the violence of the strong and armed against the feeble and defenceless . . .[1]

Tolstoy was quite as certain about the injustice of land ownership as he was about its reform. 'I agree with Henry George . . . Landlords may be expropriated without dishonesty, without compensation, as a matter of principle.' Tolstoy wrote to the Single-Tax League of Australia: 'The injustice of the seizure of land as property has long ago been recognised by thinking people, but only since the teaching of Henry George has it become clear by what means this injustice can be abolished.'

George died in 1897 from the exertions of an active mayoral campaign. James Bryce, the British statesman and writer, paid eloquent tribute to his memory. 'I recollect few things more tragic than Henry George's death at this moment, and am heartily sorry that the world has lost him. I knew him a little and respected him a great deal. He was not only a man of remarkable literary power, but a very sincere and earnest man, who has left a most favourable impression on my mind ever since.'[2] There were other tributes from Mark Twain, Sun Yat-Sen, and Lord Acton.

Winston Churchill made a thorough study of *Progress and Poverty* while he was Under-Secretary for the Colonies [1905–8]. MacLaren later saw the copy read by Churchill and noted the various underlinings of important points in the text. During this period Josiah Wedgwood, who entered Parliament in 1906 as a

---
[1] Tolstoy, L., *Single Tax*, Ch. 4.
[2] Ibid., p. 4.

single-taxer, bumped into Churchill behind the Speaker's Chair one day. 'Jos,' he told him, 'I have been reading Henry George, and I must say I can see no answer to him.'[1]

MacLaren always avoided associating the name of one man to ideas which are evident truths of Nature. He believed great ideas were timeless and immediate. For, being self-evident, they must have been observed by many in history. Indeed, George discovered and proclaimed the same ideas as Turgot, and his master, Quesnay. They in turn derived the idea of a Natural Order from ancient China. The sanction lent to great ideas derives, however, from their truth rather than their antiquity.

MacLaren was inspired by the moral courage of George in proclaiming at every season and in every climate that the freedom of mankind required only a foundation of economic justice. He had a great warmth and feeling for serious thinkers, even though he did not agree with them. He spoke often of his genuine appreciation of the character of Karl Marx and made plain his disagreement with him without ever denigrating him or his work.

---

[1] Wedgewood, J., *Memoirs of A Fighting Life*, pp. 64–5.

3

Radical Apprenticeship

Karl Marx had been a powerful weapon in MacLaren's armoury during his early debating career in Scotland. A close friend carried a copy of *Das Kapital* in a special pocket sewn into his jacket. There were a few favourite passages in which Marx dealt with the expropriation of the people from the land which MacLaren knew by heart and would regularly quote:

'Thus were the agricultural people first forcibly expropriated from the soil, driven from their homes, turned into vagabonds, and then whipped, branded, tortured by laws grotesquely terrible, into the discipline necessary for the wage system.'[1]

'The expropriation and expulsion of the agricultural population, intermittent but renewed again and again, supplied, as we saw, the town industries with a mass of proletarians, entirely unconnected with the corporate guilds and unfettered by them ... We have seen that the expropriation of the mass of the people from the soil, forms the basis of the capitalist mode of production.'[2]

Once a big-hearted Socialist was keen to let his audience know of his mastery of Marx. When MacLaren challenged him to read one of his choice pieces, he uttered only a few sentences, which clearly contradicted what he had said. Angrily, he threw the book aside and exclaimed: 'Well! I don't care what Marx says about this!'

At another meeting, MacLaren was put up to a debate on economics with the long-haired chairman of the meeting. He

---
[1] Marx, K., *Das Kapital*, vol. 1, Pt. 8. Ch. 28.
[2] Ibid., Ch.19.

was Jimmy Maxton, later to become chairman of the Independent Labour Party. Mr. Maxton made some enquiries, and realising he was to be pitted against so formidable an opponent, avoided the clash by refusing to attend.

Although MacLaren often seemed bent on fighting a moral war with the landowning class, he was careful not to attack individual landowners on a personal basis. He was opposed to the private appropriation of land value and recognised that the real support of that corrupt state of affairs was public apathy. Yet he never engaged in class politics for he felt to bring class into politics was, in Hamlet's words, 'to tear a passion to tatters, to very rags'. If class meant anything at all it was the social effect of some more profound economic cause which resulted in the maldistribution of wealth.

Around the border of the city of Glasgow a number of landowners held their land out of use. They were waiting until the growth of the city obliged the corporation to buy their land at an inflated price. To hold a city to ransom in this way was and, still is, allowed as a normal business practice in a capitalist society. MacLaren and his friends used to ask the landowners what they were paying in rates. The amount was often so derisory that the landowners usually refused to answer, the figure usually being supplied by a sympathetic friend in the rating department. One of the most notorious cases concerned the Duke of Montrose, the leader of the Glasgow Corporation. The duke claimed to own some flooded land called Loch Katrine. The City required water from the loch and the duke demanded £19,500 for the right to take water. The City Corporation was not prepared to pay such an amount, whereupon, the duke threatened to build houses around the Loch and run their sewage into it. The Corporation sued, an action which cost them £30,000. The duke eventually accepted £8000 not to poison the drinking water of the people of Glasgow. Lord Lansdowne, the landlords' leading champion, came to Glasgow to assure his audience that there was no monopoly in land. 'I deny,' he stated, 'that there is a monopoly of land. I deny still more, that it is an uncontrolled monopoly. During the last four years in England three millions of acres have been offered for sale, and in Scotland no less than two millions. I think 700,000 acres have actually changed hands in

Scotland. Well, that is hardly consistent with the theory of a monopoly. As to its being an uncontrolled monopoly, nothing is further from the truth.'[1]

MacLaren did not regard the sale of land from one owner to another as proof that there was no landowning monopoly. It was sufficient for him that the mass of the people were excluded from sharing in the value of land which they had created. By 1912, MacLaren was active, speaking at public meetings and writing newspaper articles. He attended the annual meeting of the Vacant Land Society in London, where he reported to the meeting that vacant sites in Glasgow were an eyesore; used only to dump dead cats, tyres and old tins. The air was so poisoned with chemicals that cabbages were choked as soon as they emerged from the earth. The president and founder of the Society was Joseph Fels, a tenacious American who started in commercial life as an errand boy and emerged a millionaire from the manufacture of soap. He came to England initially to develop his business but became absorbed in the land values movement and devoted his entire fortune to its work. He was barely five feet tall but his energy and enthusiasm were truly astonishing and his kindness and humour were well known. Fels purchased a 700 acre farm at Mayland in Essex and within four years it yielded livelihoods for a community of 300.

The group of land-taxers, as they were called in Glasgow, was being attacked by the Labour Party. Keir Hardy, the Labour Party founder, had said in Glasgow that the taxation of land was a dodge of the capitalist to enable him to exploit the worker with impunity, and Ramsay MacDonald, the Labour leader, advocated a scheme of land purchase. Furthermore, the local party accused the land-taxing clique of aiming to spoil their chances at a local election. In an article MacLaren dismissed such rumours of spoiling tactics as the 'conjectures of a somnambulist,' and explained that though the exploitation of workers was a fact, the evil which caused their exploitation was the taxation of everything but land values. This drew a rejoinder that MacLaren confined himself solely to land while Socialism, in its vision and emotional magnanimity, comprehended both land

---

[1] *Land Values*, January 1913, p. 37.

and capital. The socialists insisted on preserving their sense of class exploitation; it was their cutting edge. The capitalist, they believed, could well afford a land tax and, once the tax was paid, would be free to make hay with the poorer worker. Besides, they insisted, a land tax might suit an emerging society, but not one which had thousands of years of development behind it.

Before he could answer the Socialist criticism, the Liberal view of creation was expounded by Choiza Money, a Liberal Member of Parliament. MacLaren referred to him as 'that arithmetical oracle of modern apologetic Liberalism'. Mr. Money had stated that the man who lived off stocks and shares was the real target for taxation and his examination of Income Tax returns showed, he averred, that profits from businesses and professions yielded a handsome total of £350 million. While land values, he estimated, from the same returns, were worth only a miserable £90 million.

In reply to these political attacks, MacLaren claimed that man was a 'land animal', and that the land question was the foremost element of economic and social problems. Taking the example of Glasgow, he showed how a population of over one million existed on 10,000 acres, of which 3000 acres were vacant. The owners of this vacant land were waiting for the price to rise before they would be inclined to sell. These vacant sites were valued for rates at about £10,000 per acre and were assessed for a paltry annual amount of £500. If they were subject to the full rating charge, they would be valued at about £200 million and assessed for annual rates of £50,000. There was nothing in Socialist orthodox dogma to support the existence of this inhuman monopoly. The socialist insisted on taxing the capitalist but the capitalist shifted the tax by raising his prices. Thus the consumer ended up paying the taxes which the socialist had naively supposed would be borne by the capitalist. Mr. Money had misled himself by analysing Income Tax returns. MacLaren illustrated this by citing the case of Lord Salisbury's home at Hatfield. Certainly an estate of 14,000 acres so close to London was worth an enormous sum but, since it was not let out for rent, it showed in the Income Tax Returns as producing nil income. Hence, Mr. Money's estimate of £90 million was flawed. He had muddled ground rents with ground values.

Mr. Patterson, a leading Glaswegian socialist, wrote in an

article attacking the taxation of land values: 'Better the tyranny and the extortion of the landlord than the worst oppression of the money lord.' MacLaren replied by stating that the money lords' oppression was only felt after all land has been enclosed. He quoted Marx: 'Where land is very cheap and all men are free, where everyone who so pleases can acquire a piece for himself, not only is labour very dear, or is held out of use, as respects the labourer's share of the produce, but the difficulty is to obtain labour at any price.'

MacLaren went on to say, that when land is very dear, or is held out of use, then men must be unemployed. Though Mr. Patterson recommended taxation according to the ability to pay, yet he admitted that the poor cottagers and tenement dwellers have insufficient money to pay their taxes, which are paid by the capitalists who exploited their sweated labours. The remedy he proposes was that the hated capitalist pays them 'proper wages.' Yet, as MacLaren pointed out, if a dozen men are queuing for one job, why should the capitalist pay any more than he does? For wages are fixed by competition for work.

Patterson continued his attack on land taxers in a further article. He sought to show how the State 'might get back land' and put it to its best use, thereby ending the scandal of underused land. This, he revealed, could be accomplished without taxing land value; the key was the nationalisation of land. A commission would examine titles, distinguishing between villains who had acquired land by fraud or violence and those worthy souls who had acquired it by honestly earned cash. The land of the former would be taken over by the State while that held by the latter would be purchased by the State at its full value. The State would decide on the best use of land. With regard to waste land, a concession would be granted to allow owners their lifetime to bring land into use, otherwise it would revert to the State. A special tax would, however, be levied on all waste land.

He then turned to MacLaren's objections. First, as to the shifting of a land tax, he enquired whether MacLaren had ever heard of landlords increasing rent under the House Letting Acts? Secondly, he disagreed that taxes levied on capitalists were automatically recouped in increased prices. Rather, the capitalist recouped them himself by exploiting the worker. Thirdly, he questioned MacLaren's contention that when land value was fully taxed the capitalist would not be able to extort any charges. 'Had MacLaren,' he asked, 'ever heard of Trusts or Combinations?'

MacLaren responded by pointing out that the increase of rents under the House Letting Acts did not include any element of a land tax and so Mr. Patterson's points on the shifting of tax were quite irrelevant. He quoted John Stuart Mill on this point: 'A tax on rent falls wholly on the landlord. There are no means by which he can shift the tax upon anyone else . . .' He did not trouble himself with Patterson's point about the capitalist exploiting workers since it 'is quite beyond dispute that wages are fixed by workers in competition with each other; not by capitalists at all.' He was, indeed, aware of Trusts and Combinations, but not where land was taxed. He and the land taxers argued whether land value was public property and whether nationalisation was really a means of purchasing private property. Socialists had always been in favour of death duties. While these duties might recover much at death they left the causes of injustices alive. These early clashes contrasted the different approaches of MacLaren and the socialists. While the former was dealing with the foundation of society and seeking to found it upon justice the latter talked about political appearances which they rested upon public opinion. MacLaren believed the high ground of politics should be concerned with principle and not be a concourse of public consensus. MacLaren often recalled a battle at Loch Lomond. Attempts had been made to purchase rights of way leading to the shores of the Loch. The countryside around the Loch was a lung of fresh air for the population huddled in Glasgow. MacLaren was a prominent speaker at three public meetings held in Balloch in August 1911. At the first, he told his audience that it was the landlord's policy to distract their attention with talk of tariff reform and Empire. To keep men inflamed and fighting over the rivalry of King Billy and the Pope was sure to keep them occupied. On 27 August a crowd of about 5000 gathered at Balloch on Glasgow's Trades Holiday. MacLaren is reported as having given the first address. He warmed them up by saying they should regard the land value as their property; it had been appropriated by landlords. They should allow no credence to the purchase of land; no individual made it valuable and, therefore, no one had anything to sell. The land was the source of their lives and would always remain unpurchaseable. On another occasion he addressed a meeting on the shores of Loch Lomond from a rowing boat. The crowd were gathered by a wall marking out private property. MacLaren became aware of this offensive boundary during his speech. After he had worked on his audience he only had to refer to this wall, in the most lawful and casual way, to see a great cloud of dust arise where once it had stood.

In February 1912 the Marquis of Tullibardine was addressing an election meeting. Though his staunch Scottish background would normally have been enough to win votes in Glasgow, particularly since he was a Marquis as well, he went out of his way to stress his honest desire to serve working men. 'I give you men credit for being honest men and, although I am a laird and a duke's son, that is not my fault [Laughter] I hope you will give me credit for being honest. All I want to do is to work in your interests.' A heckler, called MacLaren, was becoming agitated and desired to put that touching plea to the test. 'You object,' he interjected, 'to a tax on land values?' No, the Marquis had no objection to a fair tax. Recovering himself, he said he supported a graduated income tax. But, he conceded, the difficulty was to find out what each man's income was. The heckler was not satisfied. 'The only man you can get at,' he retorted, 'is the man with land, because he cannot run away with it. [Laughter] I will watch your attitude on the Land Values question in the House.' The Marquis replied: 'Yes; watch and pray.' The two men were later to be brought together again in a fierce debate on the land question in which neither gave ground. Afterwards, despite their political differences, they became friends.

MacLaren often spoke about education and art, because he believed the capacity of art was to raise man to a higher or spiritual level of existence. One of these talks was published as an article in the *Scottish Co-operator* in July 1913:

> A people that have become insensate of all that is really beautiful, are likewise indifferent to the appeals of the idealist. To awaken the artistic sense in men and women

who are constantly engaged in the breathless struggle for a bare existence, is a task beset with difficulties, and necessitates no small measure of patience and enthusiasm. ... Art has come to be regarded as a form of amusement which can only be indulged in by men of great wealth. ... Thus art which is the soul of every democracy finds no place in the workaday existence. Contented to live in unsightly tenements in dingy streets, or penned up in some ugly factory or workplace, the toiling masses, unmindful, if not wholly unconscious, of the beauty in Nature, exist only as mere automatons empty of soul.

True, the primary cause of this extinction of the native sense of beauty is due to the vicious economic system under which they live; their natural aspirations are enchained by a ruinous and stupid distribution of the wealth they create ...

Art is not the plaything of the wealthy, but is the spirit of beauty which permeates the whole of Nature, and gives forth her message to all who can really appreciate it, make it their own, and attach their various artistic meanings to it. ... The greatness of an artist depends on selecting and interpreting whatever phase in Nature may appeal to his sense of beauty. The painter, and likewise the author, who is devoid of this selective power may succeed in giving us a very real presentment of life, but they have contributed nothing to art; they have not given their interpretation of Nature ...

In his endeavour to express his ideal of human beauty the pagan artist will adopt Venus; the medieval artist, having completed his finest effort in the creation of maternal beauty, confers upon it the title of Madonna and Child. These works of art have an affinity which transcends the popular beliefs in men and is eternal; they are embodiments of ideal beauty and the world is made richer by their presence.

His was a world in which truth and justice were buried by subterfuge, villainy, self-interest, conceits, ambitions, prejudices, superficiality and cowardice.

4

Constitutional Débâcle

From 1908 onwards the political scene in London began increasingly to attract MacLaren's attention. The rise of a new consciousness that society needed reform, a weariness with imperial pride and the popularity of Henry George's ideas – particularly in Scottish local government – exposed the ruling Tories' frailties.

Arthur Balfour who had resigned as Prime Minister in December 1905, was the last Prime Minister to resign for both himself and his government. 'So persistent, however, was Balfour's reputation for political subtlety that his resignation before an election was widely regarded as a move of surpassing dexterity.'[1]

At the end of the previous century there had been mounting pressure on the government to act on social welfare questions. In 1886 a crowd of unemployed men had gathered in Trafalgar Square. After an orderly meeting some of the crowd had run amok down Pall Mall and on to Hyde Park, smashing shop windows and breaking into carriages along the way. Three years later the dockers obeyed their leaders and went out on strike. During the winter of 1892–3 the unemployed numbered 75,000 and local authorities, although empowered to employ them on public works, could only engage 26,875.

The Empire was becoming a liability. Nothing brought this home more than the Boer War, in which a few rustic Boer farmers had defied for so long the might of an imperial power. But the war had also exposed the wretched condition of the poor. Many British volunteers had been rejected for military

---
[1] Jenkins, R., *Mr. Balfour's Poodle*, p. 11.

service because of their poor medical condition. Herbert Asquith had asked later: 'What is the use of talking of Empire if here, at its very centre, there is always to be found a mass of people stunted in education, prey to intemperance, huddled and congested beyond the possibility of realising in any true sense either social or domestic life.'[1]

At the conclusion of the war in 1904, 46,000 impoverished soldiers were interviewed. 11,000 were put on the poor law and work was found for the remainder. In 1905 local authorities were empowered, under the poor law, to provide outdoor relief – that is, relief outside a workhouse – at labour exchanges. In addition, local authorities began to provide school meals though they found it impossible to recover the costs from the parents.

Among the Empire's caricatures, such as John Bull and Empire Jack, arose Joseph Chamberlain. He argued that the Empire could be invigorated by erecting tariffs against world trade. The force of Chamberlain's argument split the Tories who traditionally embraced protectionism, particularly when it was adorned with the Union Jack. 'The triumph of protectionism,' declared Sir Henry Campbell-Bannerman, the Liberal leader, 'would set up a policy of brag and grab. The defeat of protectionism – perhaps you have it in your power to strike a smashing blow – will send forth a message of peace and goodwill.'[2]

In the General Election of 1906 the Liberal Party had fought on the issue of free trade, which had united them after their divisions of the previous century. Churchill, then one of the most radical thinkers, had left the Tories in 1904 over the issue.

The Liberals won the General Election with a majority of 220 seats over the Unionists. Among the first problems facing Campbell-Bannerman was the resolute obduracy of the House of Lords. Their Lordships seemed minded to continue Tory rule by frustrating the Commons. A Tory Member of Parliament referred to the Lords as 'the watchdog of the constitution'. Lloyd George observed more accurately that the Lords 'has become Mr. Balfour's poodle. It barks for him, it fetches and carries for him; it bites anyone he sets it on to.'

---
[1] Gilbert, B.B., *The Evolution of National Insurance*, p. 77.
[2] Wilson, J., *C-B*, p. 416.

Education was the first major contentious issue between the Liberal majority in the Commons and the Unionist majority in the Lords. For his part, MacLaren was wary of politicians handling education, fearing that students would be trained to become political conformists. But the educational system was badly in need of reform. The Churches exerted themselves to found schools for the poor so that they could teach their religion to children. The scramble was just as unseemly as that of some doctors – who became known as ambulance chasers – pursuing the sick like vultures. The government sought to loosen the religious control of schools; a move which would strike a blow to the Church of England. But the Church had long been entwined with the Tories and the aristocracy and the Liberal Bill was doomed. In 1907 the Lords amended the Education Bill so severely that it became effectively a Tory measure.

Commenting on its defeat, Campbell-Bannerman asked: 'Is the General Election and its result to go for nothing? ... the resources of the British Constitution are not wholly exhausted and I say with conviction that a way must be found, a way will be found, by which the will of the people, expressed through their elected representatives, will be made to prevail.[1]

Shortly afterwards, the Lords rejected the Plural Voting Bill, designed to end the privilege of voting in more than one place according to property qualifications. The Liberals recalled how Gladstone had been similarly defeated in his second attempt to grant Ireland home rule in 1893. The Lords also voted down the Licensing Bill on 27 November 1908 designed to reduce the number of public houses. By then it was clear that they were determined to block the legislative path of the government; the breweries and public houses had long been a power base of the Tories.

Campbell-Bannerman was determined to assert the power of an elected chamber over a hereditary bastion of conservatism. The purpose of such a constitutional revolution was not merely philosophical, however, it was keenly practical. As he explained at the Royal Albert Hall in London on 21 December 1905:

'We desire to develop our undeveloped estates in this country

---

[1] Ibid., p. 560.

– to colonise our own country – to give the farmer greater freedom and greater security in the exercise of his business – to secure a home and a career for the labourer, who is now in many cases cut off from the soil. We wish to make the land less of a pleasure-ground for the rich and more of a treasure-house for the nation.' This last sentence stood in MacLaren's mind above every political utterance; to his ears it was pure political poetry.

On 25 January 1907 Campbell-Bannerman received the freedom of the city of Glasgow. He thanked his friends, of whom MacLaren was proud to number himself. Campbell-Bannerman's wife, Charlotte, had died in August 1906. During her long illness Campbell-Bannerman had laid aside the cares of government to nurse her and her death had been a blow from which he never recovered. He died of a heart attack in April 1908, remembered as one of the most amiable of men and radical of Prime Ministers.

MacLaren observed every Prime Minister this century up to Edward Heath. Though he admired Bonar-Law and Douglas-Home for their transparent honesty he remained steadfast in his opinion that Campbell-Bannerman was of a superior order. Indeed, he regarded him as the greatest Prime Minister this century. Herbert Asquith took over and appointed David Lloyd George as his Chancellor of the Exchequer and Churchill his President of the Board of Trade. MacLaren developed a profound respect for Asquith and later for Churchill. They were determined to reduce the power of the House of Lords but they needed a bigger issue than the Education Act or a measure to abolish plural voting. After the rejection of the Licensing Bill Churchill disclosed the belligerent spirit of the government. 'We will send them a Budget as will terrify them,' he growled as he stabbed his bread.'[1]

The battle cry against hereditary rule was taken up by Lloyd George, whose oratory and wit always excited MacLaren's admiration. In a speech at Llanelli Lloyd George poured sarcastic scorn on the Upper House. Edward VII complained to the Prime Minister and Lloyd George apologised for his intemperate language. Yet only a month later he returned to this theme in a

---

[1] Masterman, C.L., *F.G. Masterman*, p. 114.

speech at Oxford. Again the King complained of this 'indecent' attack and threatened to cancel a visit to Cardiff. Lloyd George had much to gain in public estimation from a royal visit to Wales and swiftly proffered his utmost contrition.

Asquith introduced a bill for Old Age Pensions in 1908. It provided for the over 70s who were estimated to number 372,000. The pension was set at five shillings per week but did not become payable if the claimant was a lunatic, had been imprisoned during the previous ten years, or was in receipt of poor law relief. The Lords was bitterly opposed. A peer described the measure as 'so prodigal of expenditure as likely to undermine the whole fabric of Empire,' and another said it was 'destructive of all thrift.' In September 1908, McKenna, the First Lord of the Admiralty, received a surprising cable from Lloyd George asking him to build more Dreadnought battleships in the financial year to the following April. He did not much like Lloyd George and thought there must be some mistake so he asked for the cable to be repeated. It was. But battleships could not be commissioned in a matter of months. He was totally perplexed and suggested a meeting with the Prime Minister at which the Chancellor's strategy was explained.

Lloyd George would propose that the increased expenditure on national defence should be funded from a land tax. Such a plan, Lloyd George hoped, would both provoke the opposition of Lords and rally the people round a simple emotive issue. He had received the backing of Asquith who had resolved his mind firmly on the issue.

Indeed, Asquith was already convinced about the justice of such a tax. As he once said:

> The value of land rises as population grows and national necessities increase, not in proportion to the application of capital and labour, but the development of the community itself. You have a form of value, therefore, which is conveniently called 'site value', entirely independent of buildings and improvements and of other things which non-owners and occupiers have done to increase its value – a source of value created by the community, which the community is entitled to appropriate to itself ... In almost

every aspect of our social and industrial problem you are brought back sooner or later to that fundamental fact.[1]

Lloyd George presented his Budget of 1909 with provisions to tax the value of land. His speech, Hilaire Belloc remarked, 'was read from beginning to end from typewritten notes and was simply deplorable. It lasted four hours of which two and a half consisted of long stupid paragraphs about the rich being rich and the poor being poor.'[2]

There were, however, on his own backbenches, many younger members who, during the subsequent debate, forced Lloyd George to compromise. Instead of taxing the full value of land as he had wished, his Budget taxed only its incremental value through the Increment Duty, the Reversionary Duty, the Mineral Rights Duty and the Underdeveloped Land Duty.

The Reversion Duty and the Mineral Rights Duty were not taxes on land value at all. Increment Duty was a tax only on a small part of land value and was levied on death or sale. Underdeveloped Land Duty was a small tax, avoided by many exemptions, difficult to collect and impossible to understand. These duties proved cumbersome to define, expensive to administer and were repealed in 1922. Although not one of the five duties was a tax on the whole land value its opponents were able to say that the experiment to introduce land taxes had proved a total failure. This grand opportunity for reform had been thrown away and MacLaren traced the decline of the Liberal Party to their failure to deliver what they had promised. From that time it ceased to be his natural home, even though few men in public life this century have held more liberal views; MacLaren believed fundamentally that the rights of men were inherent in the nature of things and not in the petty whims of well-intentioned politicians. While the Budget was going through the Commons – a process which involved no fewer than 550 divisions – Lloyd George, speaking at Limehouse in the East End of London, made a characteristic attack on the peers and the landowners.

---

[1] Speech in Paisley, 7 June 1923.
[2] Spreaght, R., *Hilaire Belloc*, p. 223.

They [the landlords], are now protesting at paying the fair share of taxation of the land, and they are doing it by saying: 'You are burdening industry; you are putting burdens on people which they cannot bear!' Ah! They are not thinking of themselves. Noble souls! It is not the great dukes they are fearing for, it is the market gardener, it is the builder, and it was, until recently, the small holder. In every debate they said: 'We are not worrying for ourselves. We can afford it with our broad acres! But just think of the little man with only a few acres!' And much impressed by this tearful appeal that at last we said: 'We will leave him out.' And I almost expected to see Mr. Pretyman [the landlord's bagman in the Commons] jump over the table when I said it and fall on my neck and embrace me. Instead he stiffened up his face wreathed in anger and he said: 'The Budget is more unjust than ever.'[1]

Though the king protested, Lloyd George sensed that the people approved of his attack on landowners. He made a similar speech in Newcastle, telling his audience that 'A fully equipped duke costs as much as two Dreadnoughts, and they are just as great a terror and last longer.' In a rare philosophical mood he speculated: 'Who ordained that a few should have the land as a prerequisite? Who made ten thousand people owners of the soil and the rest of us trespassers in the land of our birth?'[2]

Unsurprisingly, the Lords could not stomach the taxation of their lands and they rejected the budget in November 1909, thus provoking a constitutional crisis of the greatest magnitude. How, asked the Liberal ministers, was an unelected assembly of reactionaries to determine the finances of a democratic nation?

These events in Westminster enticed MacLaren south to visit London. He sat in the public galleries of both the Commons and the Lords to witness the Tories attacking the Budget. He saw great and normally respectable peers behave with uncharacteristic venom in defence of their interests. He remembered Dr. Gore, the Bishop of Oxford, warning their Lordships that they

---
[1] Rowland, P., *Lloyd George*, p. 221.
[2] Ibid., p. 222.

would throw their dignity and sense of importance out by rejecting the Budget. During the General Election of January 1910, Churchill described their Lordships 'as meditating on their great estates, great questions of government ... all resolving the problems of Empire and Epsom.'[1] The Liberal Party won the election but their majority of 244 had shrunk to a mere two. A few months later the king died and his successor, George V, counselled a peaceful solution. A Constitutional Conference was convened with the participation of the Unionists to attempt to resolve the constitutional problem that the will of a democratic Commons could be thwarted by a hereditary Lords. The conference broke up in irresolvable disagreement in November 1910 and a second General Election was held immediately. The result was similar. The Liberals held a small majority over the Tories who, whilst considered along with the minority parties in the Commons, still held a commanding majority in the House of Lords.

Churchill had been sent to Lancashire to rove freely in order to alert public opinion to the issues at stake. Lord Curzon was also sent there to counter Churchill's campaign. Curzon cited the claim of a French historian, Ernest Renan, that civilisation was the work of aristocracies. Churchill replied: 'There is not a duke, a marquis, an earl or a viscount in Oldham who will not feel that a compliment has been paid to him. But it would be more true to say that the upkeep of aristocracies has been the work of civilisation.'[2]

Churchill published a series of his speeches during this crisis, entitled *The People's Rights*, a copy of which was highly prized by MacLaren. Churchill gave the clearest explanation of the ideas of free trade and of the taxation of land values as well as the constitutional aspects of the current crisis. MacLaren treasured and often quoted from them in the House of Commons. In 1970 he released his copy for publication.

Years later in the Commons MacLaren quoted a statement of Churchill at this time, which illustrates the latter's mastery of the land question. 'It does not matter where you look or what

---
[1] Pelling, H., *Winston Churchill*, pp. 125–6.
[2] Ibid., pp. 125–6.

examples you select, you will see that every form of enterprise, every step in material progress, is only undertaken after the land monopolist has skimmed the cream off for himself.'[1]

In another speech Churchill recounted how the poor people of south London were charged a toll to cross a bridge over the Thames. There was great agitation and the toll was relieved. The people affected were saved the expenditure of sixpence a week. However, it was observed that their rent had advanced by the same amount.

> It is quite true, [admitted Churchill], that land monopoly is not the only monopoly which exists, but it is by far the greatest of monopolies – it is a perpetual monopoly and it is the mother of all monopolies . . . We are often assured by sagacious persons that the civilisation of modern states is largely based upon respect for the rights of private property. If that be true, it is also true to say that respect cannot be secured, ought indeed, not to be expected, unless property is associated in the minds of the great mass of the people with the ideas of justice and reason . . . Fancy comparing these healthy processes with the enrichment which comes to a landlord, who happens to own a plot of land on the outskirts or at the centre of our great cities, who watches the busy population around him making the city larger, richer, more convenient, more famous every day, and all the while sits still and does nothing. Roads are made, streets are made, railway services are improved, electric lights turn night into day, electric trams glide swiftly to and fro, water is brought from reservoirs a hundred miles off in the mountains – and all the while the landlord sits still. In no great country in the new world or in the old, have the working people yet secured the double advantage of Free Trade and Free Land together.[2]

The powers of the Lords were trimmed in August 1911; henceforth they could not reject a Bill certified a Money Bill by

---
[1] Hansard, col. 563, 19:4:29.
[2] Churchill, W.S., *The People's Rights*, pp. 116–130.

the Speaker of the Commons and any other Bill could only be vetoed for two years. Their lordships assented to the Parliament Act, which contained these emasculating clauses, on the understanding that if they refused, the king would create sufficient peers to give the Bill a clear passage, in accord with his undertaking of 20 July 1911. MacLaren watched this significant event from the public gallery in the House of Lords, savouring the moment when the landowners had to yield their powers over the government's legislation.

Three Bills have subsequently passed into law under the Parliament Act; two relating to Wales and Ireland were passed by Asquith and, in 1947, the Parliament Act reduced the suspensory veto of the Lords to a year.

MacLaren was captivated by the parliamentary drama of these constitutional upheavals and sought work in London so that he could remain amongst it though he continued to visit Glasgow from time to time. He found a job as a commercial artist without too much trouble.

One afternoon he visited Tower Bridge where issues were traditionally debated in the open air. He joined the largest gathering which was being addressed by a Tory speaker wearing a boater. Evidently the crowd were sick of him and MacLaren pinned him down with questions about unemployment. He tried to evade them but eventually the crowd tired of his prevarication and he was removed from the platform and MacLaren substituted in his place. Standing before a large crowd MacLaren felt very much at home. He spoke about the constitutional question and led them in singing *the Land Song*, a well-known composition set to the tune of the *Marching Through Georgia*:

> The land, the land,
> The ground on which we stand,
> T'was God who gave the land to the people,
> Why should we be beggars with the ballot in our hand,
> When God gave the land to the people?

Years later MacLaren taunted both Lloyd George and Churchill in the Commons by quoting their former speeches, recalling them better than they did themselves. In 1928 Churchill had rejoined the Tories and was their Chancellor of the Exchequer. 'I know,' he said, 'that when people get the single tax mania in their hands – I know the symptoms well. The Right Honourable member for the Carnarvon Boroughs [Lloyd George] had a very bad dose.'

MacLaren: 'So had you.'

Churchill: 'Well, I had a slight one.'[1]

Once, in the early 1930s, MacLaren found himself walking behind Churchill in the Haymarket. He began whistling *Marching Through Georgia*. 'Have you not grown out of that MacLaren?' Churchill enquired irritably. Evidently he himself had and so he will be remembered as a war leader rather than a liberal reformer.

The valuation of land, in accordance with the 1909 Budget, was slowed down by the need to value buildings, fixed machinery and timber, none of which was liable to the tax. By 1912 the estimate that the valuations would be complete in 1914 was already beginning to look optimistic, and even if they were produced within that time many would be out of date by then. In 1912 two by-elections were won for the Liberals in Norfolk and the Potteries by land-tax candidates. MacLaren was actively involved in these by-elections. It appeared that the government had gone cold on the issue and, while professing belief in the cause of land value taxation, did nothing to expedite its implementation. In April 1915, Lloyd George suspended the fixation of final land values during continuance of the War.

The War proved to be the graveyard of Liberal principles. Upon its conclusion, as the spotlight moved from the terrible slaughter to the negotiations for peace, Lloyd George scrapped the valuation of land altogether. Later he adopted the policy outlined in the Liberal document, the *Rural Report*, which acknowledged private ownership of land and confirmed the rights of private landowners to collect rents. Going so far as to provide, in the event of a tenant falling into arrears, for the State to step into his shoes and accord the landowner an annuity

---

[1] Hansard, col. 79, vol. 213, 1928.

based on the value of his land and of the buildings on it. Though the party's *Urban Report* did attempt to distinguish between soil and site value, it is hard to believe that, in a decade, Lloyd George had betrayed himself, the Liberal Party and the supporters of his radical innovation of 1909. On 25 April 1920, while Lloyd George was abroad, Austen Chamberlain promised to repeal the land valuation provisions and to excuse arrears. Sir Alfred Mond claimed that Lloyd George had decided to repeal without even consulting Liberal Members of Parliament. Later Lloyd George explained that he had to give in to Conservative pressure.

During the General Election of 1922 a Liberal Party leaflet stated: 'the system of rating and taxing of land values have never been tried in this country . . . what are called the 'Land Value Duties' of the Budget of 1909 . . . were well meant, and they may have been sound for other purposes. But they were not Land-values Taxes.'[1]

MacLaren had seen the rise and fall of the last great moment of Liberalism in Britain. The seed planted in British soil by Henry George during the 1880s had propagated around 1900, flowered by 1907 and all but perished in the barren waste of the First World War.

---
[1] Leaflet No.2611.

5

First World War

During the autumn of 1913 MacLaren moved permanently from Glasgow with his wife and young son, Leon, to settle in Wimbledon. Fels was as impressed with MacLaren's cartoons as with his gifts of writing and speaking and introduced him to commercial artists from whom MacLaren received employment. Fels always called MacLaren 'Archie'; maybe that sounded more authentically Scottish.

He also brought him into the work of the United Committee of Land Value Taxation, which had moved from Glasgow to an office at Tothill Street, Westminster. MacLaren was busy speaking and cartooning as well as helping with the production of the Committee's monthly magazine, *Land Values*. During a visit to Philadelphia, Fels developed pneumonia and he died suddenly in February 1914 at the age of fifty-eight. His wife, with whom he had shared his interests, took over his work, but the cause had lost a tireless champion and repository of wit and enthusiasm.

In a cartoon penned at this time MacLaren gave a powerful, yet ridiculous and laughable, rendering of the human predicament. He cited a landlord wearing a shiny top hat sitting astride the globe smiling smugly while inhaling a cigar; his stomach bulging to give his fancy waistcoat the appearance of a low slung brassiere and his pockets overflowing with sacks of rent. By his side is a placard stuck into the earth reading: 'For Permission to Exist, Toil, Die and be Buried upon this Planet, apply to the Owner.' Tragedy and laughter, MacLaren used to remark, are often closely linked.

On 4 August 1914 war was declared against Germany. It was,

in the words of A.J.P. Taylor, a war 'to decide how Europe should be remade' after the break-up of the Hapsburg and Hungarian empires. 'This was no conscious aim of the combatants; they sought a new balance, a new advantage. There was jealousy of Britain's imperial possessions and her control of the sea, the French wanted to repossess Alsace-Lorraine and the Russians wanted to capture Constantinople and to control the Ottoman Straits which linked the Black Sea and the Mediterranean.' In November 1914, the cabinet admitted that its earlier prediction of a war lasting a few months was incorrect. Kitchener had startled them by predicting the war would endure for three years.

In early 1914 MacLaren joined the Independent Labour Party. Shortly afterwards, in the September of that year, he joined the Union of Democratic Control, founded by MacDonald. It demanded that negotiations be allowed to end the war and that diplomacy should be open and democratic. The organisers were pilloried as traitors; G. D. Morel, its Secretary, was imprisoned and Bertrand Russell was fined on specious charges. Its meetings were disrupted by soldiers on leave.

MacLaren became one of its leading speakers often speaking twice a week and travelling all over the country to do so. He took a leading part in opening branches at Leicester, Crewe, Kettering and Exeter. Local organisers praised the wisdom of MacLaren's speeches and his inspiration to increase their efforts for the Union. His sincerity and courage were striking. The Union had been formed to promote a democratic spirit in controlling both the war and the terms of a peace settlement. MacLaren objected to the shuffling around of men by a clique of diplomats at the Foreign Office. Many men living in poverty were summoned to risk their lives to fight a war which they did not understand only to return, if they survived, to the same depressing conditions of poverty which they had left.

He wrote to the widow of Fels in March 1915 to tell her about his work for the Union. He described how, shortly before his death, her late husband had forced Charles Masterman, a Treasury minister, to withdraw certain remarks he had made about single-taxers. MacLaren had recently attended a meeting addressed by his brother, Canon Masterman, on the subject of

'War and Democracy'. At one point the learned cleric declared that democracy was not to be trusted with international affairs as it was too ignorant! He scoffed at the notion of 'uncultured navvies seeking to control international affairs.' 'With the recollections of his brother in my mind,' wrote MacLaren, 'I could not control myself, so I got up and let him have it.' Those who knew MacLaren, even in his latter years, would attest that his outbursts of rage were like the quaking of the firmaments. He told the Canon that the navvies might become wise through their mistakes whereas the present rulers would go blundering on because their follies fell on other skins.

In an article, *The Genesis of the War*, published in November 1914 in *Land Values*, MacLaren blamed the War on the philosophies of both British and German thinkers. In Britain, Herbert Spencer and Professor Huxley, whom he called 'biological sociologists', depicted human life as a struggle between men for existence. This idea was seized upon by the monopolists to explain the existence of the most abject poverty in society. As MacLaren pointed out, the reason for poverty had been attributed by George to defective human laws and had nothing whatever to do with the innate weaknesses of either individuals or of society. By some strange perversity in human nature – or by some mental weakness – man had been willing to believe that life is not the gift of a benevolent Creator but some form of divine punishment for man's unworthiness.

German philosophy had been dominated by Hegel. His central glorification of the state was taken up by the Prussian historians, most notably Heinrich von Treiske. Hegel wanted something more grand than the creation of a German state; he wanted Prussia to rise out of its impotence to control its neighbours and then set itself up for world domination. 'War,' he wrote, 'cannot be wished or thought out of the world: therein lies the majesty of war, that the petty individual vanishes altogether before the great war of the State; war shall always recur as a terrible medicine for humanity.' These ideas had inspired Bismarck in his building of the German state.

Another historian, Frederick von Bernhardi, stated that war was 'a biological necessity.' Germany became, not a state of large and liberal principles with care for individual life, but a biological specimen, so to speak, to be analysed, classified and poked into its desired shape. The specimen could be subject to selection of a master race. Indeed Treiske encouraged all this so-called scientific poking and prodding by declaring: 'The State can do no wrong. For the State is the highest thing in the external society of men: above it there is nothing in the history of the world.'

MacLaren concluded: 'The apotheosis of the German idea is the howitzer.' The roots of the war lay in human ignorance of basic concepts of justice and freedom which in turn spawned those defective social theories. The outbreak of war was no diplomatic blunder nor an international accident. It was rather the outcome of defective thinking, particularly in the economic realm.

In April 1915 in Gravesend, MacLaren called for an end to the fighting: 'In dealing with the proposed terms of peace, now is an opportune time to open discussions on the matter and to influence the representatives of the Powers so as to enable a peace settlement to be arrived at which would make it impossible, in the future, to bring about the repetition of the awful carnage that is at present raging.'

He demanded that no province should be transferred between governments before the people had been consulted in a plebiscite. Secondly, that all arrangements should be accepted by the House of Commons before the British government bound itself. Thirdly, that the balance of power should be thrown aside and an International Council be formed to settle the quarrels in Europe. Fourthly, armaments had to be reduced by international agreement.

In a speech at York in January 1916 he enlarged on these demands. He denied the Union of Democratic Control was in any way a pro-German lobby or a 'stop the war' protest. It was a movement, supported by a cross-section of society, to extend democracy's understanding and control of war. He demanded of those who said that now was not the time to discuss these things, when the time would be ripe? It was his view that this war was a clash between privilege and poverty. The masses were generally too poor to travel to places like Germany and find out for themselves that the people there probably shared their own aspirations. In this vacuum of common understanding the Foreign Offices of both countries had channelled dealings between the peoples.

In England employment in the Foreign Office was open only to those with private incomes of at least £400 per year and who were prepared to receive no pay for the first year. It was no wonder that over half its staff were drawn from a landowning background. Such diplomats could have no idea of the lives of ordinary people. The Foreign Office should remove these undemocratic barriers and accept people on merit. The government was free to enter into agreements without consulting the House of Commons. It was a farce. Finally, he thought it immoral for private fortunes to be made from the sale of armaments. 'What would an individual coming from another planet to this earth think,' he asked, 'on seeing men working night-shifts and day-shifts, manufacturing weapons to destroy each other?' Their manufacture should be controlled by the State.

Another aspect of war which concerned MacLaren was its considerable cost. Expenditure on the war was running at ten times the normal rate of expenditure in peace-time. If the war was won, as it had to be whatever its causes, land values would rise. Did they not belong, particularly at this time, to those who created them? No, he feared, those who did not even own the few square inches covered by the soles of their feet would be taxed up to the hilt, national debt would be heaped up and unemployment would be their reward. A number of politicians, like Choiza Money and Philip Snowden, were calling for more revenue from a graduated income tax.

MacLaren worked near Victoria station. He saw young men leaving for the front with the euphoria of adventure only to return home weeks later wounded and horribly mangled. Men rallied in a mad rush to join His Majesty's colours. For most it was an escape from poverty; better to live dangerously under shell fire than endure daily life in the slums of the Gorbals. They left rotten conditions and would be lucky to return alive and unwounded. Few understood the reasons for the war, nor did they realise its cause was international rivalry over some far-off corner of the globe. 'An Englishman,' MacLaren observed, 'seems to be a sort of paradoxical figure, he is a lion when he goes to war, and a lamb when he gets home.'[1]

'Until August 1914 a sensible, law abiding Englishman,' wrote A.J.P. Taylor, 'could pass through life and hardly notice the existence of the state, beyond the post office and the policeman.'[2] The war put an end to that. Upon the outbreak of war the Dominions were committed to the struggle without their approval or even consultation. Trade and commerce were regulated, paper money was issued, merchant shipping was commandeered, the railways and the sugar trade were taken over. The mines were nationalised, wheat prices and rents controlled, cotton production restricted. By 1917 the economy was breaking down. Food and fuel were running short, trains were slow and uncomfortable, raw materials were policed, their prices controlled, and industry was directed by the State. Wages advanced only in nominal terms. National Savings were introduced. In 1918 the penny post disappeared, food rationing was introduced and there were widespread strikes. One of the earliest indications of the decline in political thought which invariably attends war is the acquiescence in the assumption of powers by the State both during the war and in the post-war economic reconstruction. A framework of society unhampered by the State, its bureaucrats and regulations, simply evaporated in the First World War.

MacLaren had registered as a conscientious objector in 1914. He detested conscription. In January 1916 Asquith, after meeting opposition on every side, introduced the Military Service Act which imposed compulsory service on unmarried men between the ages of eighteen and forty-one. By this time two and half million had already enlisted. MacLaren now had to be examined by various tribunals who would determine whether he was a genuine objector. As he later recounted, on the appointed day he went to Wimbledon Town Hall and explained his objection to the madness of war. It was pointless, he believed, to settle a dispute by blowing an opponent's head off. But he was not in the midst of fellow spirits.

The examination dragged on with both sides unable to

---

[1] Hansard, col. 508, 10:11:30.
[2] Taylor, A.J.P., *English History 1914–45*, p. 25.

understand each other. Then the solicitor on the committee, wearing a conceit of legal knowledge and replete with fancy waistcoat and silk top hat, rose to break the deadlock with an unanswerable question. 'MacLaren,' he enquired, with his thumbs poking ostentatiously in his waistcoat pockets, 'what would you do if you saw Germans attacking your mother?' MacLaren replied: 'You did not know my mother! I would ask her what she had done to make them angry.' At length they ordered him to appear before a more solemn, and no doubt more menacing, committee at Kingston. Before going in he met an objector rehearsing, in a Red Indian head-dress, his act of madness and dumb show by which he hoped to be excused war service on account of his comprehensive imbecility.

Still chuckling at the spectacle MacLaren entered the committee room. The officials were sitting on a raised table and he noticed that the hall was bestrewn with the usual artefacts of cheap patriotism – the 'vulgarities of a vacant mind', as he described them – a Union Jack and the fearsome poster of Lord Kitchener, designed to inspire either unconditional patriotism or the dread of a harrowing conscience. It worked, for the poster encouraged 175,000 volunteers in one week of September 1914 and continued to draw 12,500 volunteers a month until June 1915. MacLaren observed that the throne was as quick to associate itself with the glory of war as it would later disclaim its load of debt; after peace had been secured it would become the national debt. MacLaren looked more to the conditions of poverty in the homes of these volunteers than to the battlefields to which they were destined. Another wartime poster depicted a highlander gesturing to an empty highland glen saying 'Is this not worth fighting for?' MacLaren felt it was an alien land in which the people had no stake; it may as well have been a remote desert. The committee directed MacLaren to work in a munitions factory but he would have nothing to do with the idea. Seizing on his engineering background, they then awarded a conditional exemption from War service on condition that he become an engineer. Such a ruling allowed the tribunal to be seen as exercising authority without either having to send objectors to a work camp or to delve into judgement of an individual conscience.

Compulsory military service had failed to provide the men required since it gave rise to a large number of exceptions; every potential conscript was encouraged to find a loophole and certain work, like mining and munitions which had yielded a steady flow of volunteers, was declared essential. Monthly enlistments fell to 40,000 for the first five months of the operation of the Act; half the level of voluntary recruitment. Conscientious objectors were derided as defectives and even as traitors. 34 conscientious objectors were shipped to France and there condemned to death, though the penalty was later reduced to ten years imprisonment.[1]

MacLaren was offered a job as an agricultural engineer in Basingstoke. Almost as soon as he arrived at the engineer's premises he was introduced to the foreman. 'Are you,' he enquired, 'a member of the Amalgamated Society of Engineers?' The foreman confirmed that he was. 'Right,' said MacLaren, 'tell me when the next meeting is?' The following Wednesday, after all the mundane details of branch life had been laboriously deliberated upon, MacLaren rose to speak of wider issues. Such was the interest in what he had to say that the Society agreed to hear brother MacLaren at a special meeting. In fact, a series of meetings was arranged. They were a great success and the initial audience of about 30 grew rapidly. They did not deny that man needed air, sunshine and water in order to sustain life just as much as he needed land. Soon MacLaren was told of how the town clerk and his friends at the local hunt had taken to riding wantonly over the people's allotment gardens. To many these gardens were the only source of creative work and artistry, besides being the support of their families. MacLaren sensed the resentment of many in his audience so he became quite fulsome in his denunciations of the town clerk.

A few weeks later a man dressed in his hunting gear strode through the engineering yard. MacLaren knew by description that he was the town clerk whom he had been lashing so mercilessly for the past weeks. 'Are you MacLaren?' the local official enquired, striking his boots with his riding whip. 'MacLaren is my name, yes!' he replied. 'May I see your exemption card?' 'No, I never carry it with me.' MacLaren

---

[1] Cross, C., *Philip Snowden*, p. 145.

detested cards; men did not enter the world with cards and it was quite beyond his comprehension that they should be denied the privileges of terrestrial existence simply because they lacked a piece of paper. 'Well then, bring it to my office tomorrow,' ordered the town clerk. MacLaren agreed in such a tone that left an element of doubt in his intention.

The next day, as he approached his office, it crossed MacLaren's mind that he owed no civility to this petty official. He opened his door without knocking, sending a sentry standing inside off balance. The town clerk asked a number of questions; he seemed doubtful about the authenticity of the exemption card. But MacLaren stood his ground, much to the amusement of the sentry who clearly enjoyed seeing someone stand up to the town clerk – who had a reputation for being a bully – and was ordered from the room; having been admitted only to inspire fear in the town clerk's visitors, openly to take their side was gross dereliction of duty.

MacLaren was growing impatient to end the questioning when the town clerk unwittingly enquired about the friends MacLaren visited at weekends in London. 'Ian Macphearson, Under Secretary at the War Ministry, and Josiah Wedgwood, a commander of troops in Southern England, among others,' MacLaren replied nonchalantly. The town clerk was shaken from his provincial pedestal and mumbled something about how well his son knew Wedgwood. 'How interesting!' replied MacLaren, storming out of his office, again catching the sentry listening at the keyhole outside.

MacLaren continued with his meetings and his audiences began to entertain issues which they had never considered before. But after a few weeks he received a notice from the town clerk demanding his departure from the district on account of his 'political' views. MacLaren had been discussing natural phenomena like air, sunshine, water and land and man's basic rights to their use. Such matters were not confused in his mind, with political views. The town clerk had searched his lodgings and carefully listed the details of a few copies of Hansard in his possession and some of the sentimental religious books belonging to his dear old landlady – MacLaren described them as the 'come to loving Jesus and let him wash your tears' variety.

MacLaren had posters put up in Basingstoke for a public meeting on the night of his departure. As he approached the Town Hall he could hear the audience singing the *Land Song*. The crowd were spilling onto the pavement and he could hardly get into his own farewell meeting.

He delivered his condemnation of the War, explaining that those young men who enlisted would return to even worse poverty than that which they had left. Their poverty was but a detail in the prevailing condition of mass poverty.

He noticed four men who remained impassive while the rest of the audience clapped and cheered. He enquired who they were and his neighbour on the platform explained that they were councillors and friends of the town clerk. One of them had made a fortune out of cheap housing in the town. MacLaren silently regarded them. 'Now we will have some fun!' he thought. When he had worked the audience into a fury at the injustices connected with war and the private ownership of land value and at the juncture of both, he pointed to the four men.

> Now these four gentleman, here in the front, are living comfortably at home and sending young, trembling flesh, out to the front line, hoodwinking young men into thinking it is their noble duty to die for their country, rather than to live for the truth! Now I ask Almighty God to follow them at every step in their lives and to so curse them that while they lie on their deathbeds they may hear the screams of those men who are bayoneted at the front lines tonight.

The calm of Basingstoke cannot have been so ruffled since the days of public hangings. His denunciations set the meeting alight. When it was time to catch his train to London the audience walked with him to the station. The station master forbade them entry so a box was produced and MacLaren stood on it to bid his audience farewell. The station staff came out to listen. When the train eventually pulled away the driver sounded his whistle and the crowd cheered heartily.

When he returned to his home in Wimbledon he found his neighbour was most anxious because the police had earlier

Andrew with Stanley Baldwin

Andrew with Bernard Shaw

Andrew on his way to
Rio de Janeiro in 1929

Andrew at a gathering in the Potteries

Andrew's drawing of Neville Chamberlain after Munich

Who made the earth?

called to arrest him. MacLaren thought he had repaid the town clerk of Basingstoke adequately for the manner in which he had been expelled and that this further invasion of his privacy was just too much. He rang Macphearson at the War Office. Such was his urgent intent that he managed to get put straight through. He told him of the intimidation from the police and that if they were not instructed to leave him alone he would have a few uncomplimentary things to say in public. Macphearson had been informed of the events in Basingstoke and he advised MacLaren to keep quiet during the War. MacLaren told him directly that the last thing he or anyone else would do was to shut him up. MacLaren could tell from his voice that he had embarrassed him but this did not concern him.

Later that night the two policemen who had been at his home earlier came to apologise and pacify him. Over a cup of tea one of them told MacLaren that his own son had been imprisoned for being an objector. Having noted his son's name and the address of the prison, MacLaren assured them that his son would be released forthwith. He telephoned the hapless Macphearson again demanding the young man's immediate release. Macphearson begged MacLaren to stop being a thorn in the side of those trying to win the war. MacLaren replied that his attitude was not good enough and threatened to raise the whole issue if the boy was not home that night. 'Aye,' MacLaren later recalled, 'I said if he was not released, he risked the sharp edge of my tongue.'

Under the *ancien régime*, when French society was cowed by *lettres de catchet* and the arbitrary jaws of the Bastille, it was said that the pen of Voltaire was one of the few weapons available to the people. In much the same way MacLaren became a fearless opponent of injustice, humbug and pretension. Although it was customary to obey anyone in uniform during wartime MacLaren tended to have regard more to a person's thinking than to his wardrobe.

On 11 November 1918, Lloyd George told the House of Commons: 'I hope we may say that thus, this fateful morning, came to an end all wars.' Throughout the country people sang and danced, church bells tolled and flags were unfurled. MacLaren had a horror of war. It was a tragedy not merely on account of the harsh barbarity of men, the terrible sufferings and the futile waste of lives. The United Kingdom had lost three quarters of a million men and the Empire, 200,000, of whom almost a third were Indians. In addition there were the wounded and the shell-shocked. The greatest physical damage was suffered by the merchant navy which lost 40 per cent of its fleet. The private house building industry came to an end in 1914 and by 1919 over 600,000 new houses were needed. The railways had been overworked and were now in a poor state of repair and coal production concentrated in the richer seams.

Political thought was unhinged from its principles and wrought into whatever shape cheap popularity demanded. That is not a irreparable loss; it can be halted. But it was not. The people had lost a bedrock of principle and became gullible, sentimental and weak. They were drawn to the candyfloss and sugary confection manufactured by politicians, even though they knew it would ruin their taste and stomachs. Politicians became more concerned with presentation and less so with substance; politics had become a public relations industry.

As the twentieth century unfolded throughout MacLaren's life, the level of debate in Parliament reflected this loss of liberty and the rise of a million inconsequential schemes. In theory, Parliament is sovereign; in history it is a beacon of liberty. But in actuality it is becalmed in its own impotence, lacking the inspiration and discipline of grand ideas. Parliament is a splendid piece of machinery but the people have forgotten how to employ it to remove injustice in society.

The people have nothing more precious than their liberties. It is not Parliament nor the Constitution nor even the judiciary that preserves or enlarges them. It is their own political thinking which has won and preserved for them those liberties. Often they have suffered torture and imprisonment for their pains. Sometimes even death. Their only reward was in knowing they had suffered in order that others might be free.

MacLaren believed that when the people do not think clearly they will lose their liberties, whether to Parliament, to constitutional manoeuvres or the judiciary. Edmund Burke was of the same mind. 'The price of liberty,' he wrote, 'is eternal vigilance.' He did not refer only that of politicians, judges or leaders but to the vigilance of the people.

Burke was concerned mostly with civil liberties and MacLaren more with economic ones. Liberty cannot be categorised; it illumines man's whole existence. Civil liberty without economic liberty is like a flower without its bloom.

As mankind evolves gradually and painfully from the tribe to nationhood, thought begins to dominate action. The twentieth century opened as a century to be guided by thought yet it continued its habit of war and mindless folly. MacLaren hoped posterity would learn the futility of war.

Though the fatalities and injuries, the damage, the expenditure and the re-establishment of order are the most evident consequences of war, the degeneration of political thought was to MacLaren its most tragic legacy.

In 1914 he was thirty-one and had by then acquired his political principles. They did not become less relevant to him merely because the people had lost them.

6

Candidate for Parliament

Post-war measures are often grandly called 'economic reconstruction' though in reality they are usually a muddle-headed collection of policies presented to capture the votes of a war-wearied electorate. Shortly before its conclusion, Lloyd George declared that the war '. . . presents an opportunity for reconstruction of industrial conditions in this country such as have never been presented in the life of probably the world. The whole state of society is more or less a molten mass and you can stamp on that mass almost anything so long as you do it with firmness and determination.'[1]

The newly enacted Representation of the People Act gave almost complete suffrage to males over 21 and introduced it to women over 30 for the first time. After demobilisation in 1919 there were 13 million male and 8 million female voters. The electorate had tripled since 1914. The 'coupon' election, as Asquith contemptuously called it, returned a large majority for the coalition between the Liberals and the Unionists, which Lloyd George had proposed. Bonar Law, the Unionist leader, was a friend of Lloyd George and the idea of a coalition with him was acceptable. Lloyd George had split with the official Liberal party, which was led by Asquith. The Labour Party had returned fifty-nine members.

Dundas White, Trevelyan and Wedgwood, among other friends of MacLaren, left the Liberal Party, as MacLaren himself had done in 1914. He felt he possessed the essential principles of Liberalism but that the party had been destroyed, his sympathies remaining with Asquith, whom he admired.

---

[1] Fraser, D., *Evolution of the Welfare State*, p. 166.

MacLaren spoke during the General Election of 1918 for Richard Outhwaite in the Potteries and for Trevelyan in Lancashire. Needless to say, both candidates advocated the taxation of land values. On one occasion, in June 1919 at Burslem Stoke-on-Trent, he spoke for an hour and a half on the Coal Commission. At 9.20 pm he proposed that the meeting went on to a 'dose of economics' and his audience unanimously agreed.

MacLaren was adopted by the Labour party to stand in Wimbledon in late Summer 1919. His first meeting in the constituency, on 14 September, opened with the audience singing *Peace in our Time, O Lord* and he was 'very heartily received'. MacLaren conceded that Wimbledon had long been 'entrenched in a Tory atmosphere', but he welcomed a struggle. The war, he declared, had provided the shock needed to awaken men to the fundamental wrongs in society, but it seemed to have dispirited them.

The prevalent mood had been created largely by sentimental writers who had been touched by a comradely spirit and 'superficial casuistry' engendered by war. Great advances had been made in the science of warfare and destruction. Indeed it was an anomaly that scientists could tell with precision the nature and movements of worlds which coursed through the heavens millions of miles away but were perplexed by the existence of children walking the streets in poverty.

The difference between the study of other worlds and our own was, he felt, that in the former there were no vested interests. The private ownership of land had converted free men, providing for their own prime needs, into mere wealth producers, for in peace, the land belonged to the landlords whilst in war, it immediately became the people's to defend with their lives. But the soldiers returning from the fields of France, where they had gallantly defended the land of Britain, found the land no more belonged to them now than it had before 1914.

MacLaren concluded with the observation that the Indian people suffered more under the British bureaucracy than the Belgians had suffered recently at the hands of the Germans. The closing address, congratulating the local party on their choice of candidate, was given by Chaman Lal, a prominent figure in the Indian Congress Committee and a good friend of MacLaren's.

His next constituency meeting filled a local theatre. MacLaren warned his Tory opponent to watch out. He recounted to the 3000-strong audience how he had attended the local council meeting the previous Wednesday and had never seen such a 'sad aggregate of human beings'. They had been debating whether to pay ex-soldiers 1s 6d an hour, instead of 1s, to look after the recreation grounds. 'Up rose the wisdom of the past and said: "No!" Were these the representatives of the town?' asked MacLaren.

He spoke against a background of increasing industrial unrest. There was a railway strike in progress although a police strike had been settled. The cause of this unrest being the existence of an enormous pool of men looking for work. The Ministry of Labour had suggested that the railwaymen took a cut in wages. 'Why?' demanded MacLaren, 'Had the Duke of Westminster taken a cut in his rent?'

Turning to the Budget, he estimated that the National Debt would reach £10 billion. Before the war, it had stood at £645 million with annual charges of £24 million. Now the figures had grown to £7.8 billion and £400 million, respectively, which was nearly half the revenue. About 72% of the war expenditure of about £9 billion had been met by loans. During the war the National Debt grew fourteen times. All the while the landlord might have slept to reap the reward which his fellow men had created as land value. MacLaren gave a local example. It had been proposed to build on a 27 acre site in Wimbledon called Thomson's nursery. The owner declined an offer of £750 per acre and demanded £1150. MacLaren agreed to accept the higher figure for the purposes of levying a land tax [a cry was heard from the floor of 'that's the stuff to give 'em']. He asked his audience to support a Labour party, pledged to land taxation, at the next Election. George Lansbury, the Labour Member, also delivered a speech and Mr. Lal summed up. After the war MacLaren often took his young family for summer holidays to the Irish coast. He once related how, when on the beach with his younger son, John, the child marked out his own private domain, despite the vastness of the beach before them. Just as the tide would soon wash away this childlike boundary etched in sand, mused

MacLaren, so would political wisdom erase the private property in land value. Men want to possess, own and dominate rather than to simply enjoy and let others enjoy.

But a youthful confusion, even over the land question, did not interfere in a warm relationship between father and his sons. They were brought up to avoid religion and experts of any description and to be guided instead by natural law. MacLaren had one lasting regret as a parent. His younger son, John, showed a natural skill at drawing. Once he was having trouble drawing a man's arm and he asked his father to help. MacLaren drew the arm in with two or three strokes. His son was so astonished that what had presented so many problems was so easily drawn by his father, that he abandoned drawing from that moment on.

MacLaren attended a weekend conference to determine the Church's economic policy. He was allocated a bedroom beneath that of a bishop who seemed to spend the early hours clumping noisily around in heavy boots. Before retiring the following night MacLaren went up the bishop's bedroom and replaced his noisome boots, which he had left outside his door for cleaning, with the high-heeled shoes of a female neighbour. Thus was the unheavenly disturbance resolved.

In December 1919, MacLaren was appointed to the committee of the newly-formed Henry George Club in London. It held 21 meetings in its first year all over the country. MacLaren spoke in Glasgow, Yorkshire, Oxford, Hanley and several locations in London. He was also the guest of the Christiana University in Norway, where he spoke at Trondheim, Christiana and Bergen.

Wimbledon, however, remained deeply ingrained with Conservative instincts and MacLaren was unable to win a seat on the local council in an election in 1920. He had seen how the impetus of the land movement had come from municipal government, though not from the boroughs of complacent wealth like Wimbledon. It was a sensible step at a municipal level but it was considered too large for central government to hazard. Lacking an accompanying philosophical background of political thought, it aroused too much resistance.

MacLaren also spoke regularly for the Indian Congress Committee – which was demanding independence for India –

first becoming associated with this work in 1910. He often shared a platform with Satyamurti and Chaman Lal, sometimes in the Potteries though more often in London. He worked with Lansbury and G.B. Tillak, who had been imprisoned for his work.

MacLaren opposed the British Raj in India; it was a gross interference with the affairs of the sub-continent. The British Empire had extended the English language, introduced a railway system to India and exported a sense of public morality, but he never thought these incidental benefits justified an Empire, because Britain had never removed the social ills present in its own society. Not knowing how to order her affairs naturally, it was impertinent for Britain to pretend to govern so many others. Had it been minded to introduce reforms at home there would have been great benefit to mankind.

By 1919, India was becoming impatient with the British government's declaration, two years earlier, that independence would be granted 'at the earliest possible moment.' They had borne nearly 70,000 fatalities in the War and now were having to endure such repressive measures as the Indian Press Act, the Rowlatt Act, the horrors of the Black Terror in the Punjab and the bloody massacre in April 1919 by Col. O'Dwyer in Amritsar, when the wounded and dying – 379 in number – were given no attention by doctors or nurses. Britain had lost the allegiance of a vassal nation; she held only power.

At a meeting in the Royal Albert Hall in October 1919, even Mr. Tillak was content, as was Annie Besant, the British theosophist, to await the unfolding of the government's languid programme. But MacLaren was not. He moved an addendum to a compliant motion which demanded immediate action from the Labour Party. He associated himself increasingly with the Indian Freedom Campaign and continued to work for the independence of India right up to its advent in 1947.

Britain was also assailed at the time by the 'troubles' in Ireland. In December 1921, Home Rule was granted to the Irish Republic and though considered a fitting expedient at the time, MacLaren was not surprised that this division of Ireland gave rise to enduring problems.

MacLaren devoted four lectures in Wimbledon to the theme of 'Social Justice'. The concept had been put among the highest virtues by Plato and, later, Cicero. Yet, as they wrote, slaves toiled in conditions contrasting vividly with the immense wealth around them. Europe returned to heed their message after the Renaissance of the fifteenth century. In England, the country was being impoverished by the rapacity of its king, and people were being expropriated from their land. Thomas More wrote *Utopia* and died believing that man could progress no further. Francis Bacon taught men that to concentrate on discovering Nature's laws would lead to emancipation. Rousseau, the French thinker, sought to show that the further a nation advanced the more decadent and corrupt it became. The physiocrats proclaimed that war and poverty prevented the formation of an ideal state. They also thought that mankind had equal right to land.

Like the churches in times past, MacLaren declared, the spectre of vested interests are stamped on progressive thought and endeavour, for these interests control the chairs of the universities. They were against Labour and they also controlled the Press. In short, they had a stranglehold over society.

In another lecture, MacLaren dealt with the public apathy over foreign policy. People were summoned to fight wars, of which they understood neither the causes, nor the consequences. War was suddenly brought home to them when a knock at the door forewarned of a doorstep inquiry into the suitability of their children for military service. Even the House of Commons was unaware of the secret diplomacy which committed the government. The Foreign Office was in the hands of people who little understood the life of the people. This may have been appropriate when the people were illiterate. Poverty was the cause, not the effect, of war. MacLaren felt that the Labour Party must eliminate secrecy and root out the vested interests.

Then he dealt with the aims of the Labour Movement. If man could co-operate with, and understand the laws of Nature, he would establish social harmony both within, and between, nations. If two men applied equal effort to land and yet produced a different return, the difference was called rent and belonged to the community. There were vast tracts of land held out of use while armies of men converged on the cities to compete for work. This enclosure of land had created the capitalist system and it was futile to attempt petty reforms of it while leaving the cause of it – land tenure – untouched. The Labour party stood for free use of land, free production and the free exchange of that production. It also stood for shorter parliaments, maybe as short as two years, and for nationalisation of the railways, canals, ports, electricity and coal mines. It intended to abolish all direct and indirect taxes in favour of a single tax on land.

In another series of meetings, held on succeeding Sunday evenings, MacLaren also spoke on education and on the emancipation of women. They could not look to the Conservatives, who were the party of privilege and who had ensured that the landowners would always own the land which God had intended for the entire people. But MacLaren preferred the reactionary Tories to the Liberals, who produced high-minded ideals for consumption at General Elections but, once in office, had betrayed their principles. The Labour party had no vested interests to defend and were best placed to sweep away injustices.

Women had a definite role in a democratic party. Previously, the wealthy had considered them only as a dinner table adornment and the rest of male society tended to regard them as producers of children and housekeepers, though their poor conditions made them poor guardians of children. The moment had come for their full emancipation.

MacLaren stood in the South Park Ward in the election of November 1920 for the Wimbledon Borough Council on a platform of a new rating policy. In his last election address he gave the example of Lord Foster, who was offered £31,529 for 132 acres by the London County Council but demanded £79,000. The land was valued for rating purposes at £92! MacLaren used a poster which read: 'Vote for Mr. Blank. He Knows Where the Flies Go in the Winter.' He was unsuccessful. Wimbledon clearly was not a natural home for his thought, nor he the man for Wimbledon. In the winter of 1920/21 the post-war economic revival came to an end. By March 1921, unemployment had doubled from its level of only four months earlier. Though it peaked at two million later that June it nevertheless remained over one million throughout the inter-war years. Unemployment among ex-servicemen became a particular problem for which they were given only temporary relief. The Unemployment Insurance Scheme of 1911 which had originally provided relief to three million was extended to about 12 million males. In March 1921 the connection between contribution and benefit was severed when the Insurance Fund was empowered to borrow up to £50 million from the Treasury. Benefit was extended to two periods of 16 weeks each. This introduced the 'dole'. The insurance fund had been designed to deal with an unemployment rate of 4 per cent. In June those receiving outdoor relief peaked at over a million.

In April 1921, MacLaren was nominated by the Independent Labour Party, which he had joined in 1914, for Burslem and Tunstall. A safe seat located in the Potteries where he had often spoken in support of Outhwaite, who had gained the neighbouring seat of Hanley in a by-election.

Burslem and Tunstall was held by a Mr. Finney, the nominee of the Miner's Federation and the Federation's secretary in North Staffordshire, who was retiring. The local party wanted an independent candidate and, knowing of MacLaren's dislike of politics and of political parties, pressed him to accept. When they told him that they were not looking for a party fellow, MacLaren, who owed allegiance only to his principles and convictions, allowed his name to go forward for adoption.

Much of Labour policy seemed to have been invented to baffle everyone, candidates and electorate alike; the more there was of it, the more impenetrable it would be. Several Liberal candidates were greatly embarrassed by the liberal views of their socialist opponent, who had apparently stolen their clothes. For MacLaren supported free trade, retrenchment and land value rating; the very things they were expected to embrace for the purposes of obtaining office.

But inwardly he believed the political situation at that time was a farce. However, the local Tories sent a solidly decorated war veteran to his adoption meeting. At these meetings there is always a moment of suspense, akin to that point in a wedding service when the opportunity arises to show just cause that the couple are unfit to be married. That moment arose when the Tory rose noisily to his feet, his medals jangling ostentatiously on his chest, and demanded to ask one question of the candidate: 'What did MacLaren do in the Great War?' Before he had sat down to witness the explosion which his question would be sure to ignite, MacLaren replied: 'I tried to stop it. What did you do?' and his adversary was buried under the cheering that emphatically delivered the meeting's approval of his candidature. He was formally adopted on 2 June 1921 by the Burslem Labour Party.

Not surprisingly, MacLaren was to cause quite a stir in local committees. On one occasion, he declared of a branch resolution: 'This resolution is packed with words and lacking, entirely lacking, in clear thinking. I am sick to death of this talk about the capitalist and the capitalist system. It is not the capitalist that is at fault. What is at fault is the lack of ideas in the minds of men at this meeting.'

Commenting on the Communist State in Russia, MacLaren dismissed the Communist leaders and their writings as the 'vague generalities and the shibboleths of the ginger box orators of the last 30 or 40 years.' Quoting the nineteenth century historian Henry Buckle, he went on: 'No man that God ever made was good enough to be a dictator of his fellow men.'

In 1913 a government White Paper showed that Stoke-on-Trent covered an area of 11,154 acres, of which 5,294 were registered as agricultural land. The Borough Council which had to raise £358,619 annually took only £1,640 from these agricultural acres! Yet the ratepayers seemed to spend their time gazing at the racing pages in public houses and were not interested in taxation. Their apathy allowed Westminster to play 'Old Harry' with taxes.

In November 1921 Labour was successful in winning several seats in the municipal elections. At the celebration evening, MacLaren advised the new councillors to be wary. All could be undone when politics depended so much on changeable moods and accidental turns. Politics would always be poised on unforeseen accidents until people realised the cause of poverty. He referred to the international conference in Washington at which it was hoped there would be some international agreement on limiting armaments. There would be no agreement of real import, he warned, as long as the land question and the spectre of protectionism went unresolved. He produced a cartoon for the Washington conference depicting a naked man, labelled 'civilisation', strapped tightly to a mad, galloping black horse labelled 'armaments'. After the speech MacLaren introduced a pianist, Jeremy Hannah, to conclude the meeting; he was keen to impart his own love of music.

His Liberal opponent, Sydney Malkin, accused Socialists of being Bolsheviks and revolutionaries; people who would destroy society. Malkin was an absolute devotee of Lloyd George and would be sure to follow him however tortuous was the way ahead. He presented himself as the local man, as 'the potter from the Potteries'. MacLaren said that Stoke needed a wider perspective than a local man could bring. The people in the Potteries were governed from the House of Commons and only to a lesser extent from the Town Hall in Stoke. To the 'Bolshevist' jibe, MacLaren responded that he was a constitutionalist and never advocated reform outside the constitutional order.

Unemployment had risen and would go on rising as a result of the chaos attributable to the War, its conclusion and to the Treaty of Versailles. This grotesque treaty was observed by John Maynard Keynes who was particularly scathing of the French Prime Minister, Clemenceau, whom he described as 'possessed by one illusion – France – and one delusion – mankind.' Surely, political leaders should seek to heal the wounds of war and free trade between nations, but Lloyd George had been demanding the head of the Kaiser and handsome reparations. After two years, however, he was inclining to the advice of the Labour party who urged him to sit down with the Germans and the Russians. Having fought the war to end all wars, Britain found herself under the rule of militarism. The premier of France, M. Poincaré, threatened not to go to Washington at all if the alliances with Britain were going to be discussed in public. Trade was uncertain because many of Britain's former trading partners had learnt through the war to do without her; most notably, the Indian cotton trade had virtually dried up and Lancashire was bankrupt.

Dundas White, the former Liberal Member of Parliament,

spoke in Burslem. In economics, he pointed out, a leading principle was that supply met demand. Why then was it that there was a huge demand for houses and yet there were insufficient houses? He attacked Asquith, who had supported free trade before the war, yet had introduced 33 per cent duties on certain articles during the war and after it had condemned his measures.

Speaking directly to women voters, MacLaren urged them to take part in politics and bring with them a more human touch. He was reported as having said, '... he wanted to say to every woman that their children would have to face another drill sergeant and their homes would be swept away. There was no good mincing matters. We had just come through a war to end war, and we were now conducting international arrangements and negotiations on the pre-war lines. Everything pointed to the fresh development of another war in the near future, and he wanted women to realise what another war would mean. The next war, when it came ... would be the most terrible thing that mankind had ever known.'[1] The emancipation of the people could only come at the hands of the people themselves and that meant women had to use their vote intelligently.

The Irish question was beginning to trouble Westminster again. MacLaren thought the Irishman did not mind having his head broken by a fellow Irishman, but he would not tolerate Britain being involved. If any country on earth needed a new regime of order, based on a just system of taxation, it was Ireland. MacLaren often said the struggle in Ireland was economic and not religious; indeed he often stated there was more religion in his big toe than in all the pews of Ulster. He believed the Tories would never solve the problem by seeking, naively, to impose civil law and order over economic disorder. The two crucial elements were, first, the imposition of a just system of taxation and, secondly, a complete withdrawal of Britain from Irish affairs. The Coalition of Liberals and Tories under Lloyd George fell in the autumn of 1922, by which time it had gone further along the road toward protection. First they failed to repeal the Mckenna duties imposed in 1915 and, second, they introduced the Dye-Stuffs Import Regulation Bill in

---

[1] *Staffordshire Sentinel* 31:1:22.

a futile attempt to reorganise the textile industry. Then in 1921 the Safeguarding of Industries Bill which contained a list of key industries and products – which included doll's eyes, magic lanterns and patent medicines – and clauses to prevent dumping.

The popularity of Lloyd George as the man who won the war had faded and the country was disappointed in the social reconstruction promised by him. Among other things he had promised 'homes fit for heroes'. Indeed, they proved so inadequate that it was commonly said that one had to be a hero to live in them.

In 1922 the sale of honours by Lloyd George came to a head when a peerage was offered to a South African financier, Sir J. Robinson. His affairs had recently been the subject of litigation. Questions were raised in both Houses of Parliament during July 1922. A Royal Commission recommended that political honours should be passed to a committee of three Privy Councillors. Lloyd George had been selling honours for cash. Honours were lavished on all comers. Cardiff became dubbed as the 'city of dreadful knights'. A knighthood could be obtained for £15,000, a baronetcy for £25,000 and a barony for £50,000. Lloyd George pleaded that every party had done this. But they had used the sale of honours to swell their party funds. Lloyd George was without a party and the proceeds were credited to his personal fund which could devote its moneys to any purpose deemed by him to be worthy of support. Yet he shared the fund with his coalition partners. The Conservatives received about £3 million.[1] Yet for a conjurer like Lloyd George the plea of former usage sounded hollow.

Austen Chamberlain pledged that his party would continue the coalition after the Election. But the party were not happy to be bound by an agreement upon which they had not even been consulted. At a meeting at the Carlton Club on 19 October, Stanley Baldwin made a strong attack on Lloyd George and Bonar Law spoke in favour of ending the coalition. By 185 to 88 the Conservatives voted to leave the Coalition. Lloyd George resigned the same day.

---

[1] Taylor, A.J.P., *English History 1914–45*, p. 245.

In the General Election on 15 November 1922 the Liberal party split under the rival twin leadership of Asquith and Lloyd George. The Labour party became the second largest party. The result of the election was the Conservatives held 347 seats, Labour 142, the Asquithian Liberals 64 and the Liberals following Lloyd George 53. For the first time the Labour members represented a cross section of society. The Trade Unionists and the radical group known as the Clydesiders were diluted in the Labour Party with the arrival of the odd peer, the gentleman and middle class folk.

It was a close thing in Burslem, Stoke on Trent. MacLaren won the seat by a narrow margin. 'One of the great virtues of the Labour Party,' MacLaren insisted, 'was that there were no vested interests. He would represent the employer just as honestly as the poorest worker.' At the poll announcement a great crowd collected outside the Town Hall in Burslem and after about three hours the result was announced at one o'clock in the morning. MacLaren had won with 11,872 votes against 11,667 polled by his Liberal opponent. His majority was down almost 900 on the previous Labour majority. 'They had won the votes of the churchmen,' he boasted, 'the Wesleyians and the good looking men.' MacLaren vowed, after the poll had been declared, that above all, he respected constitutional development and he would always respect the dignity of that development in public life.

At the steps of the Town Hall he claimed victory for two ideals which were more important to him than anything else, including victories in elections. First, he would always fight militarism and war. Second, he believed the land was the property of mankind. Cheering crowds were one thing, he said, but the hope for democracy was that the mass of voters would think seriously. He was not carried away by success. He always distrusted crowd emotions; he wanted to be identified with clear thinking. He thanked God that idealism was still alive in some people; it had overcome some very unpleasant manoeuvres against him in the campaign. He was then carried shoulder high through the fog, and his supporters broke into the 'Land Song', which they continued to sing until they reached their homes.

When all the shouting was done MacLaren told a public

meeting that he had stood against drink, combines, trusts and war. But many Wesleyans had voted for his opponent, putting their thirst for beer before the economic liberty of their children. Arthur Clutton-Brock, the essayist, critic and journalist, wrote warmly in support of MacLaren contesting the Election:

> The only common will is a will for a common happiness; the rest is, like war, a delirium after which men are left weak bewildered, to recover as best they can . . . And now the cry is 'Anything for a quiet life' – in the slums. That is the cry of exhaustion after fever. . . . There is no conviction of sin, no desire of change of spirit, nothing learnt from experience, except that we must begin to save up for another fight between nations or classes, or both.
>
> Andrew MacLaren is a Labour candidate, but he is not for a war of classes or for any war at all. Behind his politics is the desire for common happiness that he would like to share. He knows that we can be happy only when all are happy together; and no man who does not know this is a practical politician.

7

Member of Parliament

MacLaren made his maiden speech in the House of Commons on 3 December 1922. Normally a new Member confines himself to felicitous statements about the beauty of a river or a mountain in his constituency and the dedication of the previous Member, whom he had been denouncing on the election hustings a few weeks before. But MacLaren was keenly aware that Parliament was the workshop where the relations between men in society were regulated by legislation and that a maiden speech was like setting to work on a blank canvas. 'Parliamentary time,' he told the House, 'can be wasted in kid-glove politics and nothing effective be done. I came to this House desiring to do something definitely along the lines of changing the law in some directions and not with the mere idea of becoming a gentleman in a parliamentary sense.'[1]

He accepted the challenge of Lord David Cecil to define the Labour Party's policy in regard to land.

> We assume, in the first instance that as man has not made the land, man has no right to establish private property in that land, which he has not made. That is the basis of our belief. It may be right or it may be wrong. I have my own private opinions about it. But on that basis we go on and say that whatever is in the land by virtue of the human community upon it, we will appropriate that for communal purposes. That is the Labour policy on the land problem.[2]

---

[1] Hansard, col. 366, 3:7:23.
[2] Ibid., col. 1694, 3:12:22.

It is doubtful whether many Labour Members had ever considered the land question and they were probably surprised that their party now had a land policy. The Speaker, Mr. Whitley, sent a note of congratulations and assured him that the House would want to hear him again. In his reply of thanks MacLaren signed himself with a deft caricature of his own head, which the Speaker's daughter preserved as a memento.

Throughout his two decades in parliament MacLaren never wavered in his stance that the land question was not a mere political question but lay at the very foundations of the existence of society. On one occasion he declared:

> It is no good saying: 'Rise and sweep all men into the Army for the defence of the country,' and then saying to them: 'After all, you are merely trespassers on the land of the country.' You cannot play with people like this much longer. Either this is the land of the people or the people are trespassers. Recently we heard Honourable Members stand up in this House and say it is dangerous that people should be allowed to walk more freely in the country. It is not dangerous to defend it; only to go about it. The week before last we were discussing the Access to Mountains Bill, all the landlords were in the House. A good many of them are here today. When we have a debate on special areas or unemployment their seats are empty.[1]

MacLaren developed a keen appreciation of the traditions of the House which concerned its procedures for the conduct of orderly debates.

> If England were to pass out of account tomorrow and become a shadow on the pages of history, the one thing which would hold her name dear to the memory of man, would be that she forged the British Constitution. The British Constitution was the contribution of this civilisation of ours to the advancement of human thought. What is implied in our Constitution? It is this, that the poorest shall

---
[1] Ibid., cols 2041–2 , 14:12:42.

be equal with the most powerful within the State to impress his or her opinion or intention upon the laws and rules of the country. It is the only instrument so far forged by man that will give peaceful evolution in society and raise men to a higher level, without disruption and rebellion. If that is destroyed, if that is sapped, if our British Constitutional practice is constantly weakened and falls to pieces, then the only thing that can take its place is blood and revolution. This constant giving of greater power to the bureaucracy, this greater control of bureaucratic machinery over the lives of our people is gradually sapping the interests of the common citizen of this country in the development of the British Constitution. That is the danger. To me that is more terrible than anything I know.[1]

He had long believed: 'Parliament was the only safety-valve against bloody revolution.'[2]

He also admired a constitutional monarchy as a much more dignified institution than a president. He was neither a critic nor an admirer of the House of Lords. It mattered to him less how the Second Chamber was made up than what interests and what ideas informed its thinking. In one debate on the Tithe Bill it was suggested in terms of awe that their lordships could staff the tribunals and that there were ex-viceroys among them. 'If anyone has ever known a viceroy,' ventured MacLaren frankly, 'who has come back from India. He will agree that he is the last man to be put anywhere, except in a museum, and behind bars at that.'[3]

T.P. O'Connor, the father of the House, described MacLaren as 'one of the artists and literateurs of his party. He is a charicaturist of talent but he is best as a speaker.'[4]

Members come to the House with little notion of the power and profundity of the simple principles of freedom and justice. Indeed, MacLaren often observed, they could not recognise a principle, even when it knocked them down in the street. He

---
[1] Ibid., col. 1880–1, 29:6:42.
[2] *Sentinel* 1:I0:28.
[3] Ibid., col. 2186, 26:6:36.
[4] *The Sunday Times*, 2:12:23.

made a point of asking new members what they hoped to achieve in Parliament, frequently causing embarrassment by so direct a question. As MacLaren observed the colour rising in their necks above their starched collars, he asked them further whether they had come to harmonise human laws with natural law or merely to pursue their own interests. Many members had an interest in representing some group, trade union or worthy cause and MacLaren agreed that Members of Parliament should represent the interests of all their constituents. But he believed that the representation of sectional groups preserved the liberties of a few at the expense of the majority. He regarded it is a fundamental axiom of politics that the only common interests of a people are its individual liberties and that the concern for this larger framework should engage political attention more than the regulations devised by bureaucrats.

It has been stated that Parliament possesses the power to pass any law save one to make black white or a man a woman. Although this may be true in a narrow legal sense it is, in any grander sense, a delusion. For natural law is, as Burke observed, moulded into the very essence and nature of things and will endure long after political parties and 'all such miserable playthings have vanished from existence.' Natural law, affirmed MacLaren, works whether or not human law heeds it, but when it goes unrecognised it can confound human law.

Speaking in a debate over the representation of university seats, MacLaren let his hair down, so to speak. 'It would be as much,' he said, 'as a man's life were worth, to tell the honest truth about economics and politics in the universities. The graduates are not qualified any more than the average man to give a special judgement on political matters. I contest the view that universities produce a type of man who is especially qualified for endowment with a second vote.'[1]

He was not in favour of remunerating politicians believing that men of character and insight needed by the State would not be miraculously unearthed by money. He himself put the welfare of society above any personal consideration; the lure of gold had neither called forth nor sustained his quest. Taking

---
[1] Ibid., col. 1381, 15:6:28.

such a detached view of financial enrichment, he was able to observe how it held others fast in its grip.

> I have had two recent experiences of the Labour Party when it was going to take office and I will never forget it. People who I used to see with red ties on, denouncing other classes, crying, 'Workers of the world unite: with nothing to lose but your chains' all this kind of stuff, and yet, when these gentlemen saw the prospect of office coming, I saw their Socialist ties disappear. I saw the sycophants queuing up, and I saw no distinction, no difference between human nature within the Labour Party and human nature elsewhere. Then why should I be told in this debate, that men who are to become Cabinet Ministers, or to hold office in a Government, are sacrificing themselves in some way or other? It is the most willing sacrifice that I have ever seen in my life. They are running up for it, saying, 'Here I am; disseminate me for £5,000 a year' ... We are told that we must do something to attract the greatest brains and the greatest ability. I would it were possible to attract honesty on to that bench, honesty that would attack the artificial causes of poverty ... Is there not a man or body of men who are prepared to lay their hands to the task of constructing this State more on the lines of God's eternal justice, or are we to believe that the best brains and ability can only be attracted if they are to get £5,000 a year?[1]

Members of Parliament were first paid in 1912 at a rate of £400 per annum. This rate was in force – apart from a voluntary drop in the early 1930s – until 1937, when it was increased to £600. MacLaren detested the notion that a politician was a professional person. His mind, in his opinion, should be filled with the needs of society.

MacLaren observed that honours had special significance for socialists. Were a heap thrown on the floor, he conjectured, among the mass of upturned backsides would be a majority of Labour Members.

---

[1] *The Evening News*, 27:11:27.

Many Members had come in search of personal vanity and the glitter of public honour. Others were diehards with no interest in upsetting the order of communal life. Poverty, they supposed, was an unfortunate reality of life and public conscience could be assuaged by heaping welfare upon the poor. The effect of mitigating poverty is, however, only to exacerbate its condition; far from solving the cause of poverty, public welfare in fact, actually worsens it. MacLaren used to illustrate this futile process of mitigation of poverty by a simple story. A poor man was sobbing with hunger in his decrepit tenement rooms in Glasgow, and some well-intentioned soul threw a loaf of bread through a roof light. The loaf broke the glass which was double the price of the loaf.

MacLaren came to Parliament to solve the miserable condition of poverty by eradicating its causes. He had specific ideas for this solution. But, as his aims were dearer to him than policies, he would have accepted a more effective idea proposed in a debate. That readiness to accept a better idea, was, to him, the real art of politics. Any idea that the art of politics consisted in clinging to power was repellent to MacLaren. What, he asked, is the use of debating an issue, when the House of Commons is more intent on winning public approval, than in doing something really useful? The only point, it seems, is to count the votes which are almost invariably known at the outset, fill Hansard with columns of ineffectual talk, useful only to put an entire population of insomniacs to sleep and to keep an army of printers on their feet all night.

MacLaren seldom tired of observing Lloyd George, the great orator of Limehouse, who was an inexhaustible manufacturer of dazzling expedients. By the time of MacLaren's entry to the House Lloyd George had fallen from power. He had missed a chance to impose a general land tax in 1909 and had launched the National Insurance scheme with a deal offering, as the slogan went, 'nine pence for four pence' when even a child knows a conjuror cannot accomplish this! He had split the Liberal Party, sold honours to line his political purse, signed the dangerous Treaty of Versailles and initiated a defunct policy of reconstruction of 'houses fit for heroes'. He was a spent force, possessed only of his native wit and MacLaren thought he should have been a comedian instead of a politician.

Once William Joynson-Hicks, a Tory Treasury Minister, was trying to define what he meant by 'increment-value' and the House were straining to follow him. The Minister had married wealth and added his wife's surname to his own in recognition of her contribution. Lloyd George leapt to the aid of a perplexed House by suggesting that, whatever the legal definition dreamt up by the Minister might be, 'increment-value' could be more readily understood as the hiatus between Joynson and Hicks!

Sitting alone for breakfast one morning in the National Liberal Club, MacLaren was asked by a waitress if he would allow a gentleman to sit at his table. He readily assented and was joined by Willie Sutherland who, according to MacLaren, ran after Lloyd George with a towel ready to dry his brow and mop his tears. Sutherland divulged excitedly that the master been up all night trying to solve a strike on the Clyde and had created with surpassing wisdom a new order, the Order of the British Empire. To ensure the compliance of the Clydesiders, he made them a sponsoring authority for this award. MacLaren, who had been through his political apprenticeship among them, knew that the Clydesiders were not to be corrupted so easily. Later on, he learned that their nomination for this august award was a most distinguished citizen who superintended Glasgow's public lavatories.

Different Members of the House would occupy themselves in various ways during debates. Churchill would construct paper triangles while Lord Hugh Cecil, whom MacLaren called the 'antique' of the House, would assiduously polish his watch chain. MacLaren passed the time amid this peaceful drama, drawing caricatures of his colleagues. He once wrote: 'There is something about a man's face, his mouth, the breadth of his head, which indicates whether he has the statesman's instincts or not. Mr. Asquith embodies that type. Mr. Churchill and Mr. Runciman are remains of it, but there are rows of men who would never appeal to the caricaturist.'

Once he drew the Deputy Speaker, Mr. Hope, or 'Old Bill' as he was known. Hardly had he finished, when Jack Jones, a Socialist M.P., seized the offending illustration and calmly walked down the gangway to present it to Mr. Hope, who was then in the Chair. The Speaker of the House is endowed with summary powers that he has accumulated through six centuries and is definitely not a person before whom personal freedom should be risked as a mere joke. Fortunately though, on this occasion, he had recourse to his humour rather than his awesome powers.

Although he brought his sense of wit to his art, MacLaren was a serious artist. 'Caricature,' he once said, 'is anything but a slapdash business. It must be proceeded by a meticulous study of the head. Phil May, for instance, often did six to a dozen studies of a subject before he produced a final sketch. The essentials of good caricature are the maximum force with the greatest economy of line. Moreover, a caricature should convey an epitome of some notable aspect of the subject.

> The best moments for a caricature are those when the subject's mind is alert and the circumstances are tense; because only when the mind is in a state of great activity does the veil fall from the passive face . . .
>
> I believe that fearless caricature is really valuable in public life. It has a greater effect than most people imagine and there should be more of it. Politicians rather like it; after all, they live upon publicity and enjoy being caricatured – no matter how severely. Politicians would rather have the stab of the cartoonist than the ignominy of oblivion. It means they have been noticed. Often when I fear that I may easily have made an enemy over a caricature I have perpetrated, the subject comes to me presently with a request that the thing is signed. Instead of the anticipated malediction I get a friendly salutation . . .
>
> There is, however, this disadvantage in the habit of caricature: it involves the continual study of heads and faces. As a result you feel yourself drawn to war, in a place like the House of Commons, with men you have never met. Your judgements of character are such that you feel you know a man before he opens his mouth! I have discussed this fact with artists, and they, especially a celebrated portrait painter, have agreed with me. The tendency makes life less comfortable if you happen to be a combative spirit . . .
>
> The face which has far more phases than that of any other

member, of course, is the face of Lloyd George. It is a face that quickly portrays the intent of his mind, and I have seen his expression flit from that of Napoleon to that of a bewildered little schoolgirl – all in a matter of seconds.

There are folk who regard caricaturists as pestilential fellows and brewers of mischief. Which reminds me of a sentence an old Irish lady used in describing men of an academic training who were bores: "They are like blotting paper; they take everything in and give out a bad impression.

MacLaren developed a short list of subjects, which included Sir L. Worthington-Evans, Baldwin, MacDonald, Lloyd George, Sidney Webb and Sir Henry Craik. There were nightmares as well; Austen Chamberlain had the chin of Lord Carson and Maxton always got muddled up with MacLaren's caricature of himself.

Several late night sittings were enlivened by MacLaren's caricatures passing along the benches. The Finance Bill of 1928, going through the Committee of Supply, was interrupted and the Speaker intervened to order the removal of one cartoon. As it was borne from the Chamber, it was cheered on all sides.

Indeed, MacLaren enjoyed an international reputation. When he visited Brazil in September 1927 a local newspaper reported: 'In the meantime, those who were near the members of the British Delegation, saw one of their members, a man with a happy face, making a caricature of the members at the Table . . . And, as the German Delegate was making his speech, the illustrious caricaturist, always smiling, commenced to make another caricature, taking the speaker for his subject. The members of the Press appreciated and commented with sympathy on the good humour of the British Delegation, always jovial and cheerful.'

One of MacLaren's most amusing studies was of Ellen Wilkinson, known as 'Sweet Nell of Red Fury', striding in a horse wig with her train being borne by a taller male with an air of consummate haughtiness which might equally have expressed the vanity of a peer or the pretension of a butler. She was paraded as an example of the new order of women.

His drawings were published in many of the leading daily and evening papers and in *Punch*. The last cartoonist in Parliament had been Sir Frank Lockwood, a generation earlier. There were many straight portraits, some amusing illustrations of grotesque ideas, some depicting the horror of war and some bringing to life the drama of the land question. MacLaren was on friendly terms with the cartoonists, Low and 'Poy', regarding them as great artists and their contribution to public life considerable. With a cartoon they could demolish falsehood or bring to life a truth which words were unable to convey with similar intensity. Humour and sarcasm was often the glove for a hand of serious intent.

MacLaren considered David Low as one of the best cartoonists at the time in England. Low, a New Zealander, had radical ideas and the London Press were initially reluctant to accept him. They were, however, soon forced to acknowledge his artistry, as his cartoons had such a deft appeal. 'Low', wrote Churchill, 'is a master of black and white; he is the Charlie Chaplin of caricature, and tragedy and comedy are the same to him.'[1] His antipodean roots made him unaccustomed to the staid, narrow view of life of the British people but he could humour them by his wicked cartoons. There was always a laughable 'sting' in his drawings. MacLaren described with delight Low's cartoons depicting the Trade Union Congress: 'A great, fat, ugly horse with great hooves, a wild look in his eye, a very small head or no head at all!' MacLaren tried to buy the original cartoon of this beast, but Low refused, telling him: 'this is my pony!' MacLaren was equally amused by Low's character 'Mr. Blimp', intended by him to represent the Tory party; 'a man with a small head, boss-eyes and wearing bathing dress.' Low stood out in dark, depressing and pompous times in the clear light of comic relief. MacLaren once described a conversation with Low, in which Low asked him how he got mixed up with Parliament instead of pursuing a career as a cartoonist himself. MacLaren replied: 'You do it with your pen and I do it with my tongue . . . Between the two of us we used to be very dangerous!' Low had destroyed Lloyd George's reputation as the leader of the

---
[1] Churchill, W.S., *Thoughts and Adventures*, pp. 29–30.

coalition after the First War by depicting him as a self-opinionated fellow in charge of a double-headed donkey.

MacLaren identified the three pitfalls of politicians as women, gold and power. He remarked how Tories were more susceptible to the first, Socialists to the second and Liberals to the third. MacLaren made many friends in the House. Many are now with him up 'yonder with the angels', as he often described the mystery of the next act.

During the 1930s, MacLaren was struck by a young member, Lord Dunglas [later Lord Home]. He evidently had an independent mind which was rare in politics. MacLaren made his appreciation plain. It did not matter to him that a man did not agree with him; it was important, however, that a Member agreed with his own thinking; instead of blindly following a party line. Lord Dunglas never seemed a Tory to MacLaren. He was also struck by his sense of humour which he shared with his brother, William. Nothing destroys pretension and humbug so effectively as humour. MacLaren's humour did not simply relieve his gravity; it often underlay it.

In the late 1950s, Lord Hume wrote to MacLaren: 'Life in the House of Commons with all its trials at that time [1938–40] was infinitely more preferable to the slogging chores of today which are all about economics which I distrust and don't understand.' Lord Home, who first entered the House in 1931, gave this description: 'I liked Andrew but did not see a lot of him. I admired his patent honesty and dedication to the cause of peace. He never allowed differing political views to interfere with friendship and this in politics is a very welcome attitude. He was always courageous in expressing his views.'[1]

MacLaren liked honesty and character in whatever party he found it and always attacked views rather than personalities. He was drawn by the honesty of Stanley Baldwin though he did not flinch from denouncing him ferociously for 'safeguarding' industry whilst also pretending to eschew protectionism.

MacLaren was not impressed with international forum. He actually saw the League of Nations at work in Geneva in 1925 where he was encouraged by the resolution of a M. Loucheur to

---

[1] Letter, 26:1:93.

appoint a committee to enquire into the economic causes of war. But he was immediately disappointed when the committee was expressly forbidden to discuss inter-allies' debts, or protection or allied armed forces, thus thwarting the whole basis of enquiry. He noted that the League suffered from a fatal weakness: that if its members discussed real questions they would undermine its existence. 'Whenever I attended the League of Nations,' he once said, 'all I could see was a lot of gentlemen watching one another to see that they did not run away with anything.'[1]

One of MacLaren's problems in the House was that he was seeking basic reform yet, as he explained:

> This House of Commons has always been afraid to challenge the root causes of the maldistribution of wealth in this society of ours. Therefore, we have a maldistribution of wealth and unjust relationships in society. The House, by the very growth of humanitarian ideas, is forced to devise this and that scheme to mitigate poverty.

Much of the time of the House was taken up with legislating over interventionist schemes – be they to protect industry, tax human labour, relieve agriculture, remunerate Ministers, to mitigate poverty or unemployment or disease, or relocate industry – which MacLaren knew would not tackle underlying causes. Whenever he spoke MacLaren tended to incur the ruling of the Speaker to stay within the narrow terms of a particular debate. On one occasion he bade the Speaker resume his seat when he was about to utter the offending word [land], because the House knew what he intended without that word being uttered. People used to complain that he only had one idea and MacLaren replied to that criticism by stating that if everyone in Britain had just one idea there would be a few ideas knocking around.

Politically, MacLaren was really a Liberal, but like others, including Wedgwood and Dundas White, he saw the Independent Labour Party become, around the First War, the more progressive force in national politics. But he owed none of his

---

[1] Hansard, 2:12:42.

ideas to the party, and regarded most Socialist policies, to do with mitigating poverty or pretending to effect social justice, as no more than sentimental claptrap devised by people who were too timid to face the underlying causes of poverty. He was always an implacable opponent of injustice and keenly aware of its consequences: '[P]overty,' he once declared, 'is not God-made, but man-made. It exists because the laws of man, made in this House, are not in conformity with God's eternal natural law.'[1]

Although strongly tipped for Cabinet rank before he was elected to the House – Bernard Shaw reckoned he would be Minister of Land – for twenty years he remained on the back benches. He had not come to Parliament for personal advance, but to fulfil that grand ambition of reforming society along paths indicated by natural law and felt that the seeking, or acceptance, of ministerial office would have muzzled his tongue. Indeed, he found it hard enough to remain a party politician, let alone a member of a government. This was because he was a thinker, perhaps even a philosopher, and in no sense could he have claimed to be a political animal. Parliament is dominated by the administration of the State and boils with party and personal controversy. MacLaren believed Parliament should set the economic framework of society and remove the causes of poverty. He was a Celt and his temperament lent passion and directness to his principles; he could almost become incandescent with rage when opposed by humbug or falsehood.

MacDonald, the Socialist leader, persisted in addressing the House as he was used to address a Socialist meeting. He tugged at his lapels and intoned: 'Ma dear friends' in his affected way. The Speaker ruled that this was not the approved manner of address in the House but he continued his unparliamentary habit, nonetheless. One day, as MacDonald gripped his coat, MacLaren swiftly stood up behind him and solemnly intoned his customary fraternal greeting. MacDonald turned, as if he had been shot in the back. Thereafter he adopted the correct procedure when addressing the House. MacLaren agreed with Voltaire when he warned against arguing with a bishop; it is

---

[1] Ibid., col. 1875; 23:6:42.

more effective to laugh at him. On other occasions, too, MacLaren brought the House down with laughter by a deft intervention. A Minister was extolling the fibre of the Scottish potato grower and declared: 'They have a hardihood which can stand ...' – Mr. MacLaren: 'Strong drink!'[1] When Neville Chamberlain was outlining some measure concerning local government he said: 'The figures that I have given indicate that it goes where we want it to go ...' – Mr. MacLaren: 'In the landlord's pocket!'[2] On another occasion, during a debate on the Budget, Chamberlain said: 'At some time or other all of us have seen and enjoyed those performances at music halls and revue where you see two artists dressed exactly alike, standing a little at the back or one side of the other ...' – Mr. MacLaren: 'Rothermere and Beaverbrook.'

MacLaren would often exchange repartee with Viscountess Astor. In a debate about the armed forces there had been much mention about their 'democratisation'. MacLaren hated these prefabricated verbs imported from America. The honourable lady was saying: 'We have to be careful how we understand this expression democratisation.' Mr. MacLaren: 'What is it?' Viscountess Astor: 'That is what I am trying to arrive at.' Mr. MacLaren: 'I think it is a horse.'

On countless occasions MacLaren reminded Lloyd George and Churchill of their statements at the time of the Budget of 1909. Many sayings had been engraved upon MacLaren's eager mind as he formulated his economic thinking. Churchill was known as the 'Woolworth Chancellor' because he was always putting taxes on womens' purses, stockings and all sorts of haberdashery. MacLaren could scarcely believe it was the same man who had earlier been the champion of justice and principle. In 1931 he expressed his failure to understand '... how this House is still fascinated by this man who can talk without reasoning!' He chided the House as 'a place of entertainment.'[3]

MacLaren seldom felt himself to be among fellow spirits. He often wished to have the ear of only a dozen or so members who

---

[1] Ibid., col. 576 vol. cxcvii.
[2] Ibid., col. 813 19:2:29.
[3] Ibid., col. 752 2:10:31.

saw things as he did. He was sure that a small body of zealots could effect a revolution that would make the French Revolution seem only a mindless eruption of violence. Once he gave himself to this sad reflection: 'I hope that what I am saying will have some weight sometimes, when one gets up in the House and makes an appeal, one wonders really whether it is only a matter of making a speech and walking out of the House again, having converted no one.'[1]

MacLaren's main concern in Parliament was succinctly formulated by him thus: 'There is no force more potent in the destruction of a civilised State than wrongful taxation, and it behoves this country to show as much wisdom in the imposition of its taxation, as I hope it will always show in its use of that taxation.'[2]

---
[1] Ibid., col. 1964–5 20:6:25.
[2] Ibid., col. 786 31:5:37

Title Deeds

Rates

Disarmament Conference

Two Prime Ministers

Churchill swimming

8

Member for Burslem

Burslem was one of the five towns of the Potteries known as Stoke-on-Trent. It had been a centre for the manufacture of ceramics and its associated crafts and artistry for time beyond memory. So renowned has the town become that a visitor might expect it to be wealthy and beautiful. Yet it is manifestly neither; rather it is a town of poverty. A few signs of splendour, like the old Town Hall, starkly contrast the dull streets. It was a challenging seat for a politician who believed the solution of poverty was the fundamental question in politics, for poverty was only too manifest in Burslem. In the Commons MacLaren referred to Stoke-on-Trent as a 'health resort'.

In 1933 J.B. Priestly visited the Potteries and wrote: 'the Potteries seem to me unique. They look like no industrial region. They are unique in their remote self contained provincialism. And they are unique in their work, and that is a craft, and one of the oldest in the world.'[1]

MacLaren was a tireless constituency member, ever ready to back a constituent against some nameless government department or raise a person who had fallen on hard times. Indeed he often demonstrated his humanity and broad sympathies best when helping individual cases.

Today a Member of Parliament is run off his or her feet by constituents complaining about their need for safer stairs, higher social security benefits, repairs to roads and buildings, and the like. His mail will amount to 10,000 letters per year, pouring in day after day, unrelenting, even during holidays. The

---
[1] Priestly, J.B., *English Journey*, p. 233.

Member has only to impress one constituent to receive letters from every aggrieved soul in the same street. He is constantly explaining an individual's rights. MacLaren maintained that this multitude of claims was born of man's failure to attend to fulfilling basic rights to life. If Members of Parliament are not prepared to address basic rights then they have to deal with millions of hard luck stories all rooted in the poverty attributable to a maldistribution of wealth. They may weep over the pitiful results of their actions, but they have not the courage to attend to the causes.

The United Committee for the Taxation of Land Values' International Conference was held in mid-August 1923 at Oxford. The main speaker was to have been Asquith. Unfortunately certain delegates, Outhwaite among them, said some ungracious remarks about their esteemed visitor. When Asquith read the newspapers the next day, he sent a telegram announcing that he would not be attending. MacLaren held Asquith in high regard. He was a scholar, concerned about the ills of society, and of such firmness of mind that he did not resile from his decisions. MacLaren went to see him at Sutton Courtney in order to apologise and beg him to change his mind. Asquith was hurt and angry and still refused to attend. Margot Asquith explained to journalists that her husband could not possibly go. She blamed certain Labour politicians but went out of her way to say that she had always liked Mr. MacLaren and respected people of definite views.

In the 1922 election, Andrew Bonar Law, though a protectionist himself, had pledged the Conservatives to rule out protectionism in the current Parliament though he intended to stay on in office only a few months because of ill health. When, in May 1923, he was diagnosed as having cancer of the throat he resigned immediately. He died five months later. His successor was presumed, on the principle of seniority, to be the Marquis of Curzon. Yet he was widely thought to be an erratic snob. A.J.P. Taylor referred to him as one 'of nature's rats'. The king played safe by calling for Baldwin. Curzon had a low opinion of Baldwin describing him as 'a man of the utmost insignificance.'

One of the measures in Baldwin's first session of Parliament was the repeal of the wartime Corn Production Act. It had ostensibly increased corn production when the Germans were sinking cargo ships. In fact it kept up corn prices and rents. At its repeal the value of agricultural land tumbled. After five months in office Baldwin, recognising that unemployment was his most serious problem, became convinced that protectionism was the best remedy. In this assumption he was misguided – though protectionism might appear an attractive device to temporarily prop up one industry or factory, it could never be a general remedy for a society. Baldwin may well have been influenced in his thinking by Lloyd George, who had recently returned from America with plans to regain office by advocating protection, knowing that if he did so he would excite the support of Austen Chamberlain and other Unionist protectionists. Baldwin boasted that his timely conversion to protectionism had 'dished "the Goat" ', as Lloyd George was known.

Baldwin confessed at Plymouth on 23 October 1923 that, in relation to fiscal matters, 'I am not a clever man.' In keeping with Bonar Law's pledge, he called a General Election before abandoning free trade. He appeared to be an honest man but he used the issue of protection to sever the sinew which bound certain party members to Lloyd George. Furthermore, he reversed his conversion in June 1924 to attract free trade Liberals. His biggest catch was Churchill – a useful figure to have on his side during the election campaign, which opened in November 1923.

MacLaren was unsympathetic to much of the official party election manifesto. He was not attracted by the programme of 'national work' on afforestation, reclamation, electrification, housing and the like, as a remedy for unemployment. He believed men wanted justice and freedom more than jobs. Nor was he keen on the War Debt Redemption Levy. He was not impressed with the Labour Party's commitment to abolish slums, because they thought this could be done by bulldozers rather than reason. He never embraced the demand to suppress drinking for he saw it as the effect, rather than a cause, of poverty. He was, though, in favour of nationalising public utilities.

During the campaign MacLaren said repeatedly that he was fighting with a Liberal programme of free trade and land value taxation. At one meeting he was supported by Josiah Wedgwood who had been a Liberal before the war. Wedgwood 'regarded Mr. MacLaren as the finest and most determined fighter there was in the House of Commons for the emancipation of the human race.'

Constantly he asked his Liberal opponent in Burslem, Alderman Robinson, to declare his policies. He had been Mayor of Stoke for three years and he professed himself an expert on housing. He contrasted his stance in the war with that of MacLaren. He had two sons fighting. MacLaren was not troubled with this resort to cheap patriotism. 'I would not talk about [housing], if I were he,' advised MacLaren, 'because he must have walked past Nile Street [in Stoke] with his eyes shut.' Having an opponent who had appropriated his programme Robinson could only denigrate the MacLaren doctrine as one of 'robbery'.

Once, when challenged, MacLaren gave his opinion of divorce. He believed that no law could hold a man and woman together and neither could the mould of marriage; only the bond of love could unite them. Speaking to a ladies meeting he said: 'At the present time no individual was in greater bondage than the working man's wife . . . Disease and slums hung together like a bunch of grapes.' At one meeting he was persistently heckled by a woman and stewards were on the point of ejecting her. MacLaren bade them leave her. 'She has a heart, like other mothers, and if we touch it, perhaps we may do some good.'

MacLaren considered election campaigns to be particularly serious occasions, for they were the times when the intelligence of the electorate was called upon. He blamed poor housing, not upon the Liberals or the Tories, 'but I am blaming you yourselves [the electorate] so long as you tolerate them. If you stand these conditions and vote for them, you deserve the conditions under which you now live, and worse.' MacLaren once observed that a man living in a state-built house needed to stretch his leg out of a window in order to have enough room to put his trousers on.

He hated heckling which, he felt, suppressed the freedom of speech and roundly condemned that meted out to his opponents. Silence during a speech and keen questioning after it were, in his mind, essential features of democracy.

In the General Election on 6 December 1923 the Conservatives lost 100 seats to hold 259, the Liberals, now 'united', won 159 seats and the Labour party won 191. No party held an overall majority, but protectionism, supported by the Tories, had been decisively defeated. Baldwin wanted to resign but the king would not hear of it. However, he was eventually voted out of office by the combined Labour and Liberal opposition in January 1924 and MacDonald became Prime Minister.

MacLaren lost his seat to the Liberals by the narrow margin of 102 votes. He was in good company, for Churchill lost too. 'I never wander through a graveyard and contemplate the epitaphs without thinking of the vanity of human wishes,' MacLaren mused, 'and in a thousand years from now no one will know who won this election.' Though he was both gracious and philosophical in defeat, he had missed the first Labour government.

Shortly after the election 221 Members of Parliament, comprising the Land Values Group, petitioned Philip Snowden, the new Chancellor of the Exchequer, for the immediate introduction of land value taxation. In March 1924 Snowden pledged to introduce the measures which they had demanded. In his first Budget that April, Snowden, an ardent free trader, repealed the McKenna import duties – which had been imposed during the War on products as diverse as motor cars, musical instruments, clocks and films – and all remaining protectionist measures. These were currently yielding only £3 million per annum. The repeal of the duties on motor cars provoked a hornets' nest among the car manufacturers and workers. Once again free trade was restored and the idea of War Debt Redemption Levy was dropped. It was a safe budget, but Snowden promised the Parliamentary Party that it was 'the prelude to the next, it is preparation for bigger things.' A strong hint that he intended to introduce a tax on land values.[1]

The London Conference on the European post-war situation was the first to admit Germany into an international forum. The Dawes Plan was ratified. This was an attempt to secure the withdrawal of the French from the Ruhr. The French had

---

[1] Lymans, R.W., *The First Labour Government*, p. 146.

occupied it, under their interpretation of the Treaty of Versailles, after Germany had defaulted in repaying reparations set at £6.6 million. 'The French,' observed Snowden, 'are very amiable when all is going their way, but unrestrained in their vituperative criticisms when they are crossed.'

Within a week of assuming office, the government recognised the regime in Russia, though MacDonald himself was not in favour of doing so. The Russians needed to raise a loan but first Britain demanded settlement of old debts. The British sought to stem the flow of Communist propaganda into her Empire. A Commercial Treaty, which dealt with trade, and a General Treaty, which dealt with settlement of debts, were drawn up. The matters covered by the latter were reserved for further talks and a credit of £30 million was granted to Russia. The Treaties became embarrassing to the government, presenting a gift to its opponents. The Liberals refused any longer to pull the oxen cart of Socialism and MacDonald now held office only by depending on the support of the Asquithian Liberals.

The two major issues before the Labour government were housing and unemployment. In response to the former it introduced Wheatley's Housing Bill which was, as Masterman observed contemptuously: 'a brilliant effort of municipal socialism.' It provided for central planning with subsidies payable in respect of rented accommodation over thirty years. It was as well that MacLaren was spared the passage of such a futile measure. He saw the housing problem as a manifestation of a deeper cause which could not be solved by bureaucrats or subsidies.

Unemployment had crept up to 23.4 per cent of insured workers by 1921 but, by 1923, the figure had stabilised at around 11 per cent. The government held back from taking action, Snowden refusing to throw money at public works.

While out of Parliament, MacLaren set up and edited the *Burslem Labour Chronicle*, which enjoyed a circulation in the Potteries of 20,000 from December 1923 to May 1925. It was a weekly paper of four, sometimes six, large pages containing political articles and comment, history, cartoons, wit and gossip. It sold for one penny and also carried MacLaren's lectures on music, notices of singing concerts and a women's column.

In one article MacLaren had criticised the local council over the remuneration of councillors. He was sued and libel damages of £100 were awarded against him. In all, he faced a bill of £1000. A fund was established and George Lansbury came to speak on its behalf. MacLaren was at least consoled by the fact that he had awakened public interest in council affairs and a group of about 30 councillors formed a 'clean government' group.

The first Labour government enjoyed only a short reign, largely though the ineptitude of MacDonald. Alexander Grant, the head of the biscuit makers McVitie and Price, had offered MacDonald a Daimler car. A childhood friend of MacDonald, Grant, transferred shares in the firm to the Prime Minister in order to cover its maintenance costs. Then, in June 1923, Grant became a baronet. MacDonald insisted, rather naively, that the present and the honour were unconnected. In fact, Grant's name *had* been down for a baronetcy before MacDonald came into power but the government's credibility was damaged.

Then, two days before Parliament rose for the summer recess, the editor of the *Daily Worker*, J. R. Campbell, a Communist, was arrested for an article which the Attorney General considered seditious under the Incitement to Mutiny Act of 1797. Campbell, however, was not a typical Communist activist, having been decorated and crippled in the War. The Attorney-General met the Prime Minister together with the Director of Public Prosecutions. There was a Cabinet understanding that the government did not want to prosecute such an untypical character and that the prosecution would be dropped. The Communist party, who were looking forward to an opportunity to discredit the government, were dismayed. They announced that they had intended to sub-poena the Prime Minister and two Ministers for the defence. Two months later, after the recess, MacDonald answered a question in Parliament about the reasons for dropping the prosecution. He stated that the matter had been the exclusive concern of the law officers and he knew nothing more about it other than what he read in the Press. The story of what actually had happened was, however, becoming common knowledge and MacDonald was forced to make a statement to the House. His 'incoherent evasive and prevaricating reply staggered the House, and made his colleagues who were sitting on the bench hang their heads in shame.'[1] The opposition, realising they had the Prime Minister gratuitously prostrate before them, pressed for a debate. MacDonald performed badly and the fate of the government was sealed. John Wheatley, a member of the government, told Snowden: 'I never knew a man who could succeed so well, even if he is telling the truth, in giving the impression that he is not doing so.'[2] Asquith spoke for many when he observed: 'I confess that it is to me, a man of rather keen susceptibilities, a melancholy thing to hear the right honourable gentleman anticipate so comfortably his own early, and indeed almost immediate, decease.'[3] Indeed, in his parliamentary experience, which stretched back for 50 years, never had a government 'so wantonly and unnecessarily committed suicide.' A General Election followed on Wednesday, 29 October 1924, the first to be covered on radio. But the campaign was marred in its last week by another blunder on the part of MacDonald. The Press published the Zinovieff letter, purported to be written by a senior Communist to his colleagues in Britain. The letter advised them to recruit Communist members among the unemployed, the military and the munitions workers and to play along with the Labour Party, as they were prepared to recognise Russia and offer her substantial loans. The authenticity of the letter was not known until in the 1990s it was proved finally a forgery. The story broke on the Saturday before the election. Yet MacDonald did not refer to it until Monday afternoon by which time the press were having a field day and the election had already been lost. The authenticity of the letter was never established but its impact on the outcome of the election was decisive.

MacLaren did, however, regain his seat. A correspondent of *Land & Liberty* reported that he had never seen such large meetings as 'Mac' attracted during the election. His victory was celebrated by a concert of classical music. In the local council elections at Stoke-on-Trent, on 25 July 1925, MacLaren also won a seat. He believed local government was the natural spring of

---

[1] Snowden, P., *An Autobiography*, vol. 2, p. 695.
[2] Ibid., p. 696.
[3] Ibid., p. 697.

new ideas on local taxation. For they were operating a rating system which all condemned as antiquated and unjust. He deplored party politics entering local government; councillors should use their own minds and be free of those political compromises, he believed. He was returned, unopposed, in the municipal elections of November 1927. Labour now held 36 out of 112 seats.

In July 1926 MacLaren censured the Stoke-on-Trent Council in the House of Commons during a debate on a Bill to detect fraud in local managers:

> I have heard much talk today and yesterday about corruption. I have some short experience of local government, and my experience has proved to me that they are not angels who go into local government, and if there is to be a searching for corruption, I am afraid the right honourable gentlemen will be very busy for the next year or so, because they will find plenty of work in putting this Bill into operation. I can tell of local authorities who are not Socialist in character, or Radical in colour at all, but for corruption, they might teach West Ham a great deal. I have been in contact with it in Stoke-on-Trent. I could unfold a tale there which would make the people in West Ham look like amateurs.

The mayor and councillors of Stoke-on-Trent were aghast at their member's temerity and publicly repudiated the remarks which besmirched their good name. MacLaren was abroad at the time, so upon his return the council resolved that he put before them his evidence. On 24 September MacLaren presented his evidence, prefacing his remarks with a robust constitutional opening. 'I want to say at the outset that, as a Member of Parliament, I am not to be threatened or intimidated for anything I said in the House of Commons, and I warn those who might know better not to attempt anything of the kind.'

He had never intended to allege that the whole of the council was corrupt, for he knew many people serving the council would be a credit to local government anywhere. He referred to two protest meetings of ratepayers in February 1925 complaining about municipal administration and the financing of the Water Board.

The *Evening Sentinel* devoted no less than seven columns to MacLaren's statement. Essentially, he was complaining that the town clerk, a Mr. Sharpley, was controlling council decisions and running the council as he wished. At a separate public meeting he used the testaments of four past mayors who had complained of much the same.

He suspected the town clerk was corrupt but could not prove it. Sharpley watched new councillors and corrupted them either by money or power or women. The wife of one of MacLaren's closest colleagues, George Greaves, recalled a telephone call reminding her that her husband, recently elected to the council, would do well to keep on the right side of Sharpley. During the Second World War, Sharpley was convicted, in his own court, of indenting for petrol rations for vehicles which he did not possess. It was rumoured that when he was interviewing bus licence applicants he would customarily leave the room during their meeting, ostensibly to use the telephone, but rather in order for payments, which would sway his decision, to be left the in the draw of his desk.

Though the Council considered it was rather excessive to ventilate his complaints in the Commons, the day was won by MacLaren.

He rarely touched on the question of religion in his political speeches; he believed that religion never mixed well with political issues. At a Citizen's Service in January 1927, MacLaren was the principal speaker.

> Christ was their ideal and example: yet after two thousand years of His teaching they found that the dominating idea in 1927 was to 'Get On – no matter how.' One man's estimate of another was too often decided by what he had got in the bank ... That day eloquent sermons would be preached in the name of Christ, the next day more rivets would be driven into the sides of new battleships, new poisonous gases would be discovered and men would do things concerning which, if they were asked: 'Is it honest?' they would reply: 'It is business.'

Once John Kearns, a party worker, asked him for his opinion on the religious aspirations of the people. MacLaren replied that they reminded him of his father's scrap metal yard – full of old bed posts and steel girders.

An outstanding character of the constituency was, to MacLaren's mind, a woman known as old Clara. She could unfailingly see the funny side of life and injected her own happiness and enjoyment into local Labour activities. She was also a robust and sincere critic but she would end every tirade with a hearty laugh. MacLaren also valued his friendships with Bill Morris, his agent, Basil Oldacre and George Greaves, both architects and local figures.

MacLaren had been fond of George V, whom he met at the opening of the North Staffordshire Royal Infirmary in June 1926 at Stoke-on-Trent. The king called himself an 'ordinary little man'. The king envied MacLaren his thick hair which shielded him from the hot sun as they stood outside. He suggested they go inside. Once there the king took out his cigarette case and offered him a 'Woodbine'.

During his years out of Parliament, MacLaren had been active in converting the Labour Party to the idea of the taxation of land values. Snowden repeated in 1927 the same pledge he had made on the subject, while speaking in Hanley, Stoke-on-Trent. He was welcomed as the principal guest at the twenty-first birthday party of the United Committee for the Taxation of Land Values in July 1928. He also circulated a pamphlet on land value taxation to 120 delegates at the Labour Party Conference in October 1928.

In April 1928, Baldwin, the Prime Minister, visited Stoke-on-Trent to open a new system of gas manufacture. The visit had been arranged by MacLaren. Baldwin described that he had turned on taps and pushed buttons, which, for all he knew, might have blown up half the town and probably give rise to a paragraph in the local paper, headed 'Another of the Prime Minister's Blunders.'

MacLaren proposed the toast of the Prime Minister and his wife after a lunch in the Town Hall. 'I cannot resist the temptation of saying that, although our politics may be of different colours, I have a very warm place in my heart for the present Prime Minister ... He was a member of the House of Commons and he never forgot that. He had the attitude which makes one see nothing but the clouds and forget that one was walking on earth.' MacLaren recalled how, when he had been in a nursing home recovering from an operation in 1922, Baldwin had sent him a book with a personal note. The Prime Minister began his reply to the toast by jokingly expressing the hope that saying that MacLaren was a friend of his would cause him no damage in his constituency. He then went on to praise the traditions of the Potteries.

There were, in fact, murmurings about MacLaren's friendship with the Prime Minister. Petty minds disliked Socialists fraternising with Tories. Normally these mean sentiments wither of themselves, but they were embraced by an official of the local Labour Party who pursued his quibble in a letter to the local press. He maintained that MacLaren should not have associated with the Prime Minister's visit. 'I have never believed,' MacLaren responded, 'that it is good to hate a man with whom you do not agree. I have believed in fighting to the bitter end, even your best friends, on a matter of principle, when that matter is really vital ... I am here to meet his policies and slash them, but that does not spoil the friendship which exists between us. We, the Labour Party, have lost nothing, but we have gained by displaying a certain amount of liberality of thought.'[1] The murmurings rumbled on throughout the summer and in October MacLaren replied to critics. They attacked him for having supported the Council for conferring the freedom of the city on the Prime Minister. MacLaren was unmoved by threats to withhold union affiliation fees. 'I would fight the division tomorrow, if told to, with nothing. ... (the) critics. ... not one of them could stand being looked at for five minutes. He referred to them as 'a coterie of bloodless effigies'.[2] He intended to abide by the divisional Labour Party and to put the Central Labour Party in their place if they interfered.

Unfortunately, his colleagues were not willing to be so magnanimous and the Stoke Central Labour Party met to oust

---
[1] *Evening Sentinel* 7:5:28.
[2] *Birmingham Gazette* 18:10:28.

MacLaren, summoning him to answer eight charges in an indictment. The 'prosecution' would speak for thirty minutes and he would be allowed thirty minutes for his reply. Then the officials would sit alone to consider their judgement before delivering their sentence. The charges related to MacLaren's fraternisation with Baldwin, to his regret that party politics had been introduced into municipal affairs, to his exhortation that politicians should leave business alone and his general attitude towards the Labour Party, apparent in several speeches, which were considered anti-socialist.

MacLaren declined the invitation to appear, arguing that all complaints should be made through the local Burslem branch. On 17 October the Divisional Labour Party in Burslem met in Tunstall Town Hall. In front of an audience of 1000 MacLaren spoke for an hour and half replying to eight charges made by the Central Party about trivialities. He spoke of jealousy within the Central Party. He was accused of being an intellectual. He denied that he was one. People preferred 'variety to verity'. He said that he started life as an artist and judging from the 'cramped mentality of politicians' he wished they had been artists too. For they might have some vision. He was in politics to tell those who put him there that they were as important as he. He was quite happy to leave politics if told to by the rank and file provided that his replacement was as competent as he. The Central Party called in a National official, J. Compton MP. He attended a meeting at which the indictment of charges was read out. When he realised that MacLaren was to be tried in his absence he declared the meeting 'irregular'.

The Burslem branch had already refused to come under the jurisdiction of the Stoke Central branch, and this had caused a continuing feud within the party. Eventually the National Executive stepped into the row, in the person of Arthur Henderson who was often wheeled out to settle fraternal disputes. So much so that he was known as the 'oil can' because he got the party machinery moving again. He was also, incidentally, a fervent advocate of land value taxation. He delivered the appropriate remedy and referred the relationship of a central body, like Stoke Central Labour Party, to a branch body, after Burslem, to the National Executive of the Labour

Party. A private meeting was held for an hour and a half in Burslem Town Hall under the chairmanship of Henderson. It ended with a vote of confidence in MacLaren. The dispute was the first in a series of public quarrels between MacLaren and George Meir, the Secretary of the Stoke Central Party, which persisted throughout the next decade.

The Burslem seat was not highly prized among Conservative candidates, being considered more a training ground than a winnable marginal. But the experience of standing against MacLaren was undoubtedly a salutary one. His opponent in the 1929 election, A. Harrison, took the usual party line and ventured out like a good Conservative with his Union Jack, having digested the Conservative propaganda thoroughly. During questions at his first meeting an elderly woman asked if God had made the land for the people? Knowing there was a strong Methodist presence in Burslem, he readily agreed with that naive, but charmingly innocent, proposition. Whereupon the assembled audience sprang to their feet and roared: 'Why haven't we got it?' The party briefings lay uselessly on the table before him as he struggled to reply.

During the campaign MacLaren travelled on a train carrying football supporters to a Cup Final. He described the spectacle as 'damnable'. What would happen when this great game was over, he mused, and the 20,000 fans were hoarse through shouting. Some would miss the last train home and some would be bailed for disorder, but the directors would count their receipts. MacLaren was haunted by crowds of football supporters in the later years of his life, as he lived in a studio close to Craven Cottage, home of Fulham Football Club. 'I never look at a crowd coming out of a football ground without getting afraid of democracy,'[1] he often remarked.

He once spoke up for Rev. J. Wilson, Vicar of Sneyd, one of the few local clergyman prepared to go on a public platform and speak the truth fearlessly. Apparently, he was being ostracised for doing so. 'Father Wilson would be a nice clergyman if he went to teas in the afternoon and engaged in small talk. If he went to garden parties and spoke to ladies about sewing matters

---

[1] Hansard, col. 1569, 2:7:31.

the chances are that he would be a Bishop in a fortnight but he has a nasty habit of talking about tyranny.'

The intervening years of Conservative government up to 1929 saw momentous events; the bungled attempt to restore the Gold Standard, the defeat of the General Strike, the emergence of Keynes with his idea of state spending, the arrival of Sir Oswald Mosley and John Strachey in the Labour Party with their mania for State planning and the formation of economic interventionists among the Tories. From 1925 MacLaren constantly harried Churchill for his budget measure to de-rate agricultural and industrial land. It being pretended that this would ease the burden on industry when, in fact, it had the effect only of swelling the landlords' rent by a commensurate amount.

Snowden knew a different orthodoxy and dismissed all this new thinking as moonshine. All passed under the rule of Baldwin and his government of 'old men'. Baldwin appeared not as a clever politician but as a plain man of simple, old English tastes. The General Strike in May 1926 arose out of a dispute by the miners. It lasted nine days and left the nation stunned. MacLaren saw the episode as an exercise of political power without regard to economic reality; the outcome of the puerile doctrine of class consciousness.

When a Trade Union Bill was introduced in the following year, MacLaren said:

> You might as well, try to pitch back the Atlantic Ocean with a fork as try and stop a national strike by that Bill. Men went on strike because their wages were too low, their hours of work too long or because they felt some injustice had been committed against them. Strikes were becoming more prevalent as men became more intelligent and the more they saw the contrasts in society.[1]

In 1929 the Local Government Act abolished the Poor Law Unions and the Guardians. The necessary reform, to MacLaren's mind, was to abolish the cause of poverty not the starched-collar army of mitigators. Their abolition under the Act signalled only

---
[1] Evening Sentinel 2:5:27.

a move to make the mitigation of poverty a national rather than local problem.

Baldwin denounced the old Socialist cry for the nationalisation of the means of production, distribution and exchange as the old battle cry of politicians untrammelled by responsibilities.

The General Election in 1929 was fought largely on the issue of unemployment which was than running at a million. The Socialists had no specific remedy for the problem but they gained 288 seats in Parliament, which exceeded those won by the Conservatives by 28.

At a victory celebration party MacLaren gave voice to his disquiet about France's attitude towards Germany. The breakdown of the Paris Conference was, he feared, a way France had sought to make a demonstration which would intimidate Germany into disgorging reparations. 'We are faced with the possibility of the entire central parts of Europe plunging headlong into discord.'

Back in his constituency MacLaren took an interest in many things besides politics. He was delighted with the Labour Party's parties for poor children and a newspaper noted that one New Year party for 500 children in Tunstall Town Hall ended with the children taking home a large apple, an orange and a packet of sweets. It reported that, though their clothing bore evidence of their poverty, they were clean and their faces were bright. In particular he was a keen supporter of the Burslem School of Art. He was impressed with their spontaneity and originality which invigorated the design of pottery in the district. He observed that the students worked well together and that there seemed to be no spirit of jealousy evident in their work. In particular he paid tribute to Major and Mrs. Frank Wedgwood for cultivating this humility in the students.

In October 1927 he opened an art exhibition in Burslem. 'If men were to be successful in their efforts to conquer the forces of Nature,' he said, 'they would be forced to produce something beautiful.' He well remembered discussing the point with Joseph Conrad, who pointed out the beauty of a sailing ship – 'beautiful, and compelling admiration.' MacLaren observed:

that men had to adapt the vessel to comply with Nature's rules and regulations, with no room for fancy ornamentation ... We cannot look back 20 or 30 years ago without feeling that [our forbears] were obsessed with the idea that a thing was a work of art, only if it was ornamented with whirligig lines – ornamentation which had no relation to the thing to which it was attached ... Art meant lovely cities, beautiful cities and proper social conditions, but these, again, could only spring out of some new idealism.[1]

Perhaps it was a long way off yet, but he thought he was right in saying that: ' ... everywhere men were for new ideals, examining old faiths, the old religions and philosophies, and finding some of them wanting.' He hoped that this would ' ... lead to young people who were pupils of such schools as that [the Burslem School of Art], trying to appreciate the beauty that God had given us in the creation of mankind, because it was only in the marvellous creation of the earth that they could really learn the history of Art itself.'

MacLaren also played a major role in the construction of St. Joseph's Catholic church in Burslem, which Arnold Bennett intolerably called 'the church of genuflections'.

I went into the church one day when it was being built [MacLaren recalled], and while I was there Father Brown looked in. I suggested it what a nice idea it would be if the ordinary people could paint and decorate the church and make stained glass windows reminiscent of the Middle Ages, and said it would better than professional machine-made attempts at decoration.

Father Brown protested that they had no money with which to do the decorations, and was apprehensive of my idea that we should send some students to the art school to learn this work – pottery workers, miners, teachers and shopkeepers. Finally, however, he agreed and these local folk have been working for a year cutting the windows and stained glass in the form of Normandy slabs. The glass is

---
[1] The Sentinel, 18:8:27.

similar in colour and texture to the glass now to be seen in Chartres Cathedral. There were many burst fingers and cut hands when they started, but they did not mind these casualties. Now they have completed four windows based on cartoons drawn by Gordon Forsyth. . . . The brickwork is the finest I have seen. It has all been supervised by Father Brown himself. He would not agree with my idea that no plaster should be used in the interior of the building but that pure coats of whitewash should be used as you have in the Scandinavian and Free Reformation churches. This allows the texture of the brickwork to show through the white. He only agreed with my suggestion when I assured him that plaster work was the work of a hypocrite to hide bad workmanship. The roof was composed of 200 square feet of wooden panelling and beams . . . To enter the church is to feel transplanted into a Spanish church of the Middle Ages.[1]

The church was said to look like a Cathedral when it was opened in May 1927. The roof of the Lady Chapel carried a lifelike figure of the Madonna and Child, and in the side chapel there was a life-size panel of St. Joseph and the Child. The roof of the baptistery was an excellent piece of design and colour, the canopy of the font bore the symbolic dove carved in oak.

'There has been such an extraordinary interest in this church building by the local folk, that they have learned to appreciate art and the beautiful,' declared MacLaren, 'that they are beginning to feel that they do not want to live in slums, but have beautiful houses and surroundings.'

The church was consecrated by Cardinal Bourne who noted the unique way in which it had been constructed. When he went to open other churches he usually found that the architect lived in London or that the paintings came from Italy. But here, in Burslem, the church had been built entirely by the people of Burslem.

---

[1] *Daily Dispatch Stoke* 11:5:27.

9

Ducal and Shavian Interludes

In December 1925 the Duke of Northumberland admitted to a parliamentary committee that his royalties from coal mining amounted to £75,531 gross [£35,831 net]. He was asked for his comments on the case of a Kent landowner who suddenly had found himself richer by almost £4000 a year merely because he permitted a mining company to dig for coal on the land which he owned. His Grace was astounded that such an impertinent question should be addressed to him. 'Are you suggesting,' he enquired incredulously, 'that I am not entitled to receive this?'

MacLaren seldom quarrelled with landowners. They were often not the most articulate or disputatious breed and their most effective defence was to hold their tongue. Instinctively, they tended to agree, to allow this impudent mountebank MacLaren, dubbed McClarity, to get his radical ideas off his chest. But on this occasion MacLaren saw the duke's astonishment as an opportunity to publicise the question.

The duke had stumbled clumsily into the public eye. Landowners were expected to exact their toll on society quietly as they had done for centuries. To expose oneself to radical Members of Parliament from the other party was inept and without consideration of the whole class of landlords. The duke had in several speeches been likening the Labour Party to a bunch of Bolsheviks and hoodlums.

The most striking physical dissimilarity between MacLaren and the duke was in their profiles. The duke had a chin which retreated to his neck, whereas MacLaren's head was dominated by his chin which gave his countenance rock-like confidence. The duke's expression was one of studied disinterest with regard to any particular subject, idea or person; it seemed only to concentrate itself when attempts were made to confiscate his modest receipts of royalties. Then it became distinctly vulpine.

MacLaren sent an open letter to the duke laying down the principles which entitle any person to claim anything as personal property. The duke replied.

8 January 1926

The Duke of Northumberland thanks Mr. MacLaren for his letter. The Duke entirely agrees that 'the working classes can read, think and draw their own deductions'. It is precisely for this reason that he feels convinced that they will not put up much longer with their present so-called leaders.

He ventures to point out that no working man capable of serious thinking would assert that 'the title deed to a property is based on a labour effort which established it' – an assertion which is as contrary to common sense as it is to every law, human and divine.

Moreover, if it were true, it would justify not the confiscation of the landowners' wealth, which is the product of the labour, public spirit, and devotion to duty of many generations of landowners, but of the Labour Party Funds, which are the product of legalised extortion and organised deception.

Nor would any educated working man ask the Duke such a question as whether he made the land. He would know that the prairie value of land is nil, and that its present value has been created mainly by the labour, the enterprise, intelligence and capital of the landowner.

Nor would such a working man deny the obvious truth that the King, as head of the State, was entitled to grant the land to those best able to look after it – a denial which evinces total ignorance of the historical and ethical foundations of civilised society.

Above all, no working man capable of reasoning at all would assert that the robbery of the landowner would not impoverish the State. Every Board schoolboy knows it would result in national bankruptcy in a week, owing to the destruction of the whole credit system of the country and of security for all property of every kind.

These few instances will suffice to show that Mr. MacLaren has not read or thought sufficiently about the subject to draw intelligent deductions, and he cannot therefore be qualified to represent the working classes, who, as he rightly points out, have learnt to do so, and who, in spite of the teachings of Labour leaders, still respect the Eighth Commandment.

MacLaren was now beginning to warm to the correspondence. He replied:

11 January 1926
Your Grace,
I thank you for your gracious reply to my letter. It is not couched in a tone which would lead me to believe that you are calmly reasoning over the propositions I placed before you, and which I asked you either to deny or substitute by some other moral and rational arguments which would support your claim to the land now in your possession.

You say that no working man capable of thinking would assert that the title deed to property is based upon a labour effort. This is an assertion, you say, which is contrary not only to common sense, but to every law, human and divine.

Would you please show what is the basis upon which should rest any claim to private property? It is not enough to deny my proposition. You must put something more substantial forward as an argument in support of your position.

The origin of property
If I appropriate the wages of one of your agricultural labourers would he be right in arguing that I had stolen his property because I had taken from him that which was the result of his labour effort?

Is there a law in the country, whether 'human or divine', that would support me if I said he was making an 'assertion which was contrary to common sense', and that therefore I had the right to claim his wages?

We can only have a property claim to things produced by

human effort, and individuals who claim things as property must prove that in some way or another they have rendered a labour effort to establish their claim to that property.

This seems to me to be the very foundation of any moral claim to property. I sympathise with you in your position. You find yourself to be the owner of land and all the mineral wealth embedded in this land. You never made the land, nor have you exchanged anything produced by your labour with the person who did make it, nor has it been freely bequeathed to you by anyone who had a moral claim to it.

You know these things as well as I do. An elementary acquaintance with history shows that the origin of all property in land was robbery, on the part of a few, of the common rights of the people.

Do you deny that all men have equal rights to life? If you do not, do you agree that if I have an equal right with you to live, that therefore I have equal rights with you to use the land which is the very basis of human existence?

If I am debarred from making use of the land by some private interest, is it not clear that the actions of these interests are denying me my right to life?

You have told the Commissions that you allow other people to use your coal and your land. This is tantamount to saying that in your powers as a landlord you can deny other men the right to use God's earth.

You speak of the land as 'the landlord's wealth', which is the product of the labour, public spirit and devotion of duty to many generations of landowners. Your economics are a little antiquated here. Land is not, and never can be wealth. *All wealth is the product of labour applied to land.* Land is the source from which all wealth springs, and I want you to prove that the labour, public spirit, and devotion of you and your forebears have ever created an acre of it.

What about the rent?

If you find my proposition difficult to meet with logical argument, pray do not transgress good taste by making such a libellous and insulting statement, that the Labour Party

Funds are the product of legalised extortion and organised deception. Although this statement can be applied to every penny of rent now exacted by landowners from those who use the land, I did not think of applying it until you had a fair chance to prove your case.

You say that the present value of land has been mainly created by the labour, the enterprise, intelligence, and capital of the landlord. Now, supposing the landowners did 'labour' and had 'enterprise', and the other quality, do you say that the value of the land which now comes in to you in enormous annual fortunes would be the same in amount if all those people who are not landowners were to leave England tomorrow?

It is because the value of the land rises in proportion to the growth and demands of the population, and is therefore a communally-created value which belongs to the people, that I am pressing you now in order to stop your 'enterprise' in carrying out the legalised extortion and organised deception of landlordism.

I reassert here what I said in my first letter, that no King or government can abrogate the right of posterity to the use of land by creating immoral title deeds and conferring them on landowners.

Finally, I am conscious enough of my own inability to advocate the rights of the people to the land. I am anxious that gentlemen like you should show me and my colleagues in the Labour Movement where we err in the claims we make. The Eighth Commandment, of which you remind me, says 'Thou shalt not steal'.

It is in order to find out who is the transgressor against this moral law that I beg you again to cast aside aspersions upon your political opponents and show us, by reason and that intelligence which you have told us you possess, why it is that although God made the land for the people, you have it and they have not.

This correspondence also caught the imagination of Lansbury, who challenged the duke to a public debate. But the duke had been on stage too long and declined in the following terms:

21 January 1926
The Duke of Northumberland has received Mr. Lansbury's letter of January 18. He regrets that he cannot entertain the proposal to take part in a debate on the morality and equity of land ownership as no section of public opinion worthy of any consideration questions it. To do so would mean questioning the right to own a suit of clothes or a pair of boots.

The Duke will always be glad to debate the subject of land ownership with anybody who shows an elementary knowledge of the subject, who represents any section of opinion worth considering, and however fallacious, are at least plausible enough to warrant serious attention. These conditions are not fulfilled by Mr. MacLaren, and if his views are shared by Mr. Lansbury and his friends, the proposal amounts to an invitation from an insignificant society of robbers to debate the morality and equity of the Eighth Commandment.

Such a debate would be a futile waste of time, and to broadcast it would be an insult to the public. Nor does the Duke feel justified in meeting, in what would appear to the public to be a form of friendly rivalry, persons whose views are subversive of all civilised government and society.

Lansbury did not often come across a landed and belted duke and could not resist attacking the noble rear as it fled the controversy. He wrote:

21 January 1926.
My Lord,
I am in receipt of your letter of January 21, which, if you will permit me to say so, is quite typical and worthy of a man whose whole existence from the day of his birth till now has depended on the inherited right of his parents and himself to rob, plunder, and exploit the workers of this land. I admire, and I am sure all those who read your letter will admire, your audacity, insolence and courage. You are saying what many others of your class would like to say, but lack the brazenness to say.

This however, does not excuse your impudent assumption that your title to own thousands of acres of land and extract toll from the labour of others who risk life and health in getting coal is on all-fours with the right of a poor man to own his clothes or to own a piece of land which out of his own hard earnings he has bought and paid for. You and your class never earn one penny, never intend to earn one penny, but have lived and still live on the proceeds of other people's labour. When I was a boy your family and others of our *old Nobility* plundered the citizens of London of millions of pounds simply because those citizens desired to improve the centre of our great city. Northumberland Avenue and the adjacent land was formerly enclosed as the ancestral home of your house. You know perfectly well what it was valued at for rateable purposes, and you know too the extortionate rate at which citizens of London had to buy out what were called the rights of your family. You know as well as I do that the value which attached to the land which is now Northumberland Avenue was a value which neither you nor your ancestors ever did a days work to create. It was the presence of population, the needs of the people that gave value to that land: but you and other robber Lords of Britain have got away with and are still living on the swag.

You dare not take up the challenge of Andrew MacLaren, not because we are an insignificant society of robbers – you know we are not – but because you belong to a small but very powerful society of robbers, who exist by the forbearance of the people. You dare not stand before a loudspeaker and claim that you directly or indirectly earn a single penny of the tens of thousands you draw in mining rents and royalties: you dare not stand before a loudspeaker and say that you or your forbears ever did a useful day's work to create the value of the land for which the citizens of London paid tribute to your family two generations ago.

You claim that rents, royalties, way leaves, must be the first charge, and that these must be paid even if the worker starves. You have great impudence, but I suppose it is a sign of grace that you have not enough impudence to make so barefaced a claim in the hearing of millions of your fellow countrymen.

One word more. Don't imagine that you can defend your land ownership, you who call yourselves the noble families of Britain. Many of us have read your histories: we know from whence you came – the choppings and the changings, marryings and inter-marryings, and we know, too, that a very large proportion of you would, if you belonged to the labouring classes, be described as the children of bastards. The governing classes should never have allowed us to dig into history and read from the records of the 'noble houses' of this country. A king's kept woman bears him a child – and behold a new duke or earl. Indeed, this is nothing when we look at records of murder and violence which constitute the history of the legitimate families. People who suffer, as our aristocracy does, from the disadvantages of a criminal ancestry, often also from intermarriage and degeneracy, have claims on our sympathy, and we do not expect in their public remarks the intelligence shown by an ordinary worker. But there are limits to our tolerance.

Although you have not the courage to come to a public meeting, such a gathering will be held. We will leave a place for you on the platform if at the last moment you can pluck up enough courage to come and face a public audience and defend your position. If not, judgement will go against you in your absence.

George Bernard Shaw had evidently been amused by this incident and he wrote to MacLaren:

10 February 1926
My dear MacLaren,
I am frightfully tempted to disguise myself as the Duke and wipe the floor with you. But what should I do if he were to turn up? On the whole I think I shall be safer at home.

However, the meeting will be a glorious lark; and if I were young enough for such games I should certainly join you for the fun of the thing.
Ever,
G. Bernard Shaw

The dismissal of the Labour Party in such right-wing terms might be delivered safely in the precincts of White's Club or on the grouse moors of a fellow landowner. But in the plain light of day they caused a great deal of amusement.

Speaking in York on 26 January J.R. Clynes MP said that far from the Labour Party being packed with insignificant robbers, it was apparent that a growing number in the Party were motivated to end the landowner's robbery which had gone on for centuries.

On 26 January the Daily Herald printed these verses. They were written probably by Lansbury:

I rebuke,
Said the Duke
With his hand on his heart,
The Socialist brigands
Who question my right, as
A Duke to the earth:
It is no subject for mirth:
It is a libel!
Why look at the Bible!'
But suppose the Book
Read too far in that book . . .'

Garrit Johnson, a well-known publicist in California, wrote in early 1918 to Bernard Shaw to tell him of attempts to reform the rating system by a tax on the rent of land. He was impressed with Shaw's *Fabian Essays* and thought he could count on his support. But, surprisingly, Shaw withheld it and even damned Henry George's formulation of the law of rent.

Johnson sent Shaw's letter to MacLaren, who had known Shaw as a passionate advocate of the precise use of language on the question involving the law of rent. Indeed on one occasion, Shaw had cautioned MacLaren not to waste his time talking to people who had not understood the law of rent.

What follows are the slightly abridged versions of the correspondence between MacLaren and Bernard Shaw, which was published under the title *The Rent of Ability*.

9 July 1918.
Dear Mr. Shaw,

I have just read a letter of yours in *Everyman* [Los Angeles] in which you express your views of the single tax and its propaganda, and I feel that it cannot be allowed to pass without some comment.

You hint in a general way, that by virtue of a varied and exciting pilgrimage into the fields of abstract economics you were cured of all your earlier illusions as to the proposals of Henry George. 'I had no sooner swallowed *Progress and Poverty* than I went on to Karl Marx and Proudhon,' you say. Now what it was you derived from your reading of Marx and Proudhon which improved upon *Progress and Poverty* you do not say. It is an old trick to say: 'Oh, I am aware of such and such a point in economics, because I have read *Das Kapital*.' This is an effective extinguisher for those whose sole mental equipment is the stock-in-trade shibboleths of their party. But you cannot ride off on this hobby-horse quite so successfully ... Bald assertions are never satisfying, it matters not who makes them ...

Henry George's statement of the law of rent, and of its relation to other economic factors, sheds more light upon the poverty problem and its solution than all the metaphysical and cumbrous tomes thrown on the weary world by Marx, Proudhon and Co.

There is no socialist in England who has equalled you in lecturing others upon the importance of a clear understanding of the law of rent. You have twitted Mr. Mallock and socialists for still floundering on the wrong side of this *pons asinorum*, yet you tell us that you went on from *Progress and Poverty* to Karl Marx and Proudhon! Did Marx or Proudhon understand the law of rent any more than Mr. Mallock? ...

At the Fabian Summer School last August, I asked you ... if Karl Marx clearly saw the law of rent: and you manfully admitted that he did not.

In view of this fact and considering the importance which you rightfully attach to a proper understanding of the law of rent, why do you place such stress on the works of Marx and Proudhon? I suspect that you appreciate their writings only as they lend colour to your own fanciful notions of what you term the 'rents of ability and capital.' The old terms 'wages' and 'interest' are not sufficiently exciting to find a place in Shavian economics, therefore we must wipe them out and place that which they previously connoted in the category of Rent; having performed this feat we have settled all squabbling over matters concerning the just awards to the individual and to capital, and cleared the path to state socialism.

'Henry George,' you will say, 'has proved beyond all doubt that no individual has a moral right to appropriate the value arising from the use of land; it is communally created and belongs in justice to the people as a whole. I extend this principle to the value of ability and capital, and maintain that the people as a whole ought to appropriate all the values of capital and ability, because without the presence and demands of the community, ability and capital would have no value. It is upon this ground that I demand the state distribution of income.' . . .

You complain that Henry George made no provision for the socialisation of these 'rents of ability and capital'. That is true. To those of us who have studied *Progress and Poverty*, and not merely 'swallowed' it, no such provision is necessary. We know that the mere ownership of capital and ability cannot empower man to enslave another where land is free. If this fact escaped you when you swallowed *Progress and Poverty* it must be self evident to you if your mind still retains the pronouncements of Karl Marx. Furthermore, where land is free opportunities will be opened whereby men will be able to develop whatever abilities they possess, and men with marked ability would win their awards not by privilege and monopoly but by the value of the services they rendered to a free community.

Coming to the physiocrats, you say: 'Now, Voltaire, in the pamphlet entitled *L'Homme aux Quarant Ecus* quite easily smashed Mirabeau.'

Did he? Have you not read the reply which one of the physiocrats made to Voltaire? I believe it was Condorcet who effectively smashed Voltaire in the foreword and notes to the *Tale of the Man of Forty Crowns,* which are to be found in the edition of Voltaire published by Kehl. Voltaire was a great satirist, but a very poor economist.

In the last part of your letter you have plagiarised a slur which is neither true nor germane to the subject of your note. 'The single tax,' you say, 'was advocated by capitalists who opposed socialism and who saw the advantage to themselves of diverting attention and taxation from their enormous gains to those of the landlord.' This statement is neither true of the past or the present!

If you wish to discredit single tax it is open to you to do so with all the intellectual powers at your command; but to resort to methods of mud slinging is a procedure which I least expected from you. It was only last August I heard you advise the Fabians to read *Progress and Poverty*, and you were lavish in your praise of Henry George. After so short a period your abuse of those who have been true to George's principles is somewhat perplexing.

Even though it were true that the taxation of land values was approved by wealthy capitalists, would that disprove the genuineness of the single-taxers' aims? Would it be a fair argument to maintain that socialism is a snare for the docile masses simply because it is advocated by wealthy capitalists, aristocrats and successful playwrights? I am sure that on reflection you will admit that such modes of 'argument' are unworthy . . .

Again, you say Marx's description of land civilisation as 'capitalism in its last ditch' was not unprovoked. Now, quite apart from what ever may have given Marx provocation to throw this aspersion upon George's propaganda, it is incumbent upon you at least to be in keeping with the facts before you reiterate such a statement. How many of the capitalists in Great Britain can you write down in black and white who are known to be single-taxers? Have the capitalists of today or at any other time clamoured for the taxation of land values? I have been for a number of years associated with the movement and what I have experienced is this: but for a number of zealous students, mostly men of the office and factory, devoting their spare time to the study and propagation of single tax principles, the ideas of Henry George would have little influenced the political thought of this country. True, a few wealthy men subscribe to the leagues, but with as pure and disinterested motives as you have when you subscribe to socialism. I will venture that for every one wealthy supporter the single tax movement has in Britain there are a dozen supporting bureaucratic Fabianism.

Finally, you suggest the single taxers' demand for the opening up of the land for the people is an agitation quite a century and a half out of date; will this be your reply to the soldiers when they come back from the battlefields where they have re-established their claim to the use of their land?
I am, yours sincerely,
Andrew MacLaren.
17 July 1918

17 July 1918
Dear MacLaren,
Keep calm; and do not suppose that this is a question of the authority of George or of Marx or of Proudhon, and that it can be settled one way or another by abusing them. Marx, when he wrote the first volume of *Das Kapital* clearly had no more grasped the law of rent than Ruskin had. George, when he wrote *Progress and Poverty*, had not seen that the rent of land was only a form of a much wider category of economic rent. It is therefore idle to suppose that any conclusion George and Marx arrived at within these limitations can be workable.

The practicable way to deal with the question is to take any statistical estimate of the economic rent of this country or any country in which there are returns like our income tax returns available for such estimates. Then face the question of what would happen if these were, by the operation of a single tax, thrown into the Treasury. What would the Treasury do with it? What would be the effect if the Treasury sat on it and did nothing?

I have not read the notes by Condorcet to which you

allude, and am much interested to know that they exist. What is the date of the Kehl edition or translation? Of course Voltaire was not, for modern purposes, an economist. Neither was Condorcet. Neither, indeed, was Adam Smith or Turgot; for the law of rent was not worked out until the days of Ricardo, Malthus, Anderson and West; and its extension to certain forms of personal ability and villainy, which has assumed such monstrous proportions in our time, was not worked out until the American economist General Walker handled it. No one doubts that if it be true that one acre of cultivable land may, by virtue of its fertility or situation, produce ten times as much as another, it is no less true that the same acre of land in the hands of one man may produce a hundred times as much as it will produce in the hands of another, and that in the hands of certain sorts of men (higher mathematicians or Rodins for example) it will produce just nothing at all.

Finally I am not mud slinging when I state as a fact, which I leave you to find out from your own experiences, that men who can handle capital, when they can be brought to understand the single tax propaganda are quite prepared to support it as a means of relieving their taxation at the expense of the landlord. Why should they not? It is true that most of the capitalist single-taxers I have known, from Walker of Birmingham to Fels, have believed that land nationalisation would automatically abolish poverty without touching capital. But the fact remains that they would not touch capital. Again and again in the Fabian Society we could have enlisted rich men if we had consented to allow them to join without committing themselves to the part of our basis which included rents other than those of soils and sites. In America the distinction is positively rampant. I do not see why you should object to having attention drawn to this sort of support if you believe that a single tax on rents of soils and sites will solve the social problem. In that case I am doing you a single service.

And if you do not believe it, what on earth are you quarrelling with me about?
Yours sincerely,
G. Bernard Shaw

In fact the assertion by Shaw that the so-called Law of Rent was first discovered by Henry George does not accord with the historical fact that it had been comprehensively understood by Turgot in the second half of the eighteenth century. Rather than call it a law, Turgot maintained that it was a natural self-evident truth. The reason for interjecting with this observation is not only to state the falsity of Shaw's remarks, in so far as they applied to Turgot, but also to emphasise their truth in respect of the others whom he mentions.

14 August 1918
Dear Mr. Shaw,
... Your remark, that George, when he wrote *Progress and Poverty*, 'had not seen that the rent of land was only a form of the much wider category of economic rent' expresses the immediate point at issue.

Candidly, I cannot see what is gained, in so far as a clear understanding of economics is concerned, by this ingenious extension of the term 'rents' to the returns of ability and capital. Furthermore, there is a subtlety about the process of reasoning as exemplified in the writings of Say, Mangolt, Herman and Walker, which makes me a little suspicious of the object they had in mind when they widened the application of the term 'rent'. The law of rent as propounded by Anderson, Ricardo, and developed by George, was by its very simplicity and practicability dangerous in the extreme for the future of landlordism; it concentrated the attention which would bring the final assault. But the professors, true to their scholastic tradition, set to work to bury a simple conception in the dust of metaphysical jargon. They declared that the 'rent of land is not a thing by itself, but is the leading species of a large genus'; that differential values are not peculiar to land, but are equally expressed in the returns appropriated by the owners of capital, and individuals of marked ability. In this they made the best of the hint Stuart Mill gave them when he said:

'All advantages, in fact, which one competitor has over another whether natural or acquired, whether personal or the result of social arrangements, assimilate the possessor of the advantage to a receiver of rent.'

This generalisation of the theory of rent was a heaven sent blessing to the vested interests. By the introduction of this analogy between land values and other values, together with a naive insistence upon the words 'differential revenues', the fundamental distinctions between land on the one hand and capital and ability on the other, were entirely ignored. It is not surprising to find that this theory had a ready acceptance among the economic professors; it gave them a safe subject for unending dissertations which savoured of much knowledge and ample erudition.

But you and your colleagues in the Fabian Society were not to be undone by the complexities of the schools. No, you have accepted this smug theory of rent, and with the hilarity of pilgrims in a new paradise you wring your hands for joy and proclaim Professor Walker and the other 'rent of ability' theorists as the great geniuses who have evolved a new economic formula which substantiates all that socialism has stood for.

But to do justice to Walker, I don't think that ever he suspected that a theory of collectivism would be founded upon his analysis of rent. Even Marshall seems to have had a fear of extravagant deductions being made from this rent analogy when he said: 'Land and human beings differ in so many respects even that analogy, if pressed very far, is apt to mislead; and the greatest caution is required in the application of the term rent to the earnings of extraordinary ability.' . . .

It is quite obvious that unless the analogy was pressed to extreme limits, just as you and your colleagues have pressed it, there could be no justification in economics for the state appropriation of the returns of ability and capital. But no amount of ingenious manoeuvring with economic phraseology is ever likely to overcome the just claims of the individual to the full enjoyment of whatever he has produced as a result of his own labour and skill.

The basic error in your reasoning is that, I think, due to a belief which you have, in common with all schools of socialism, that the power to enslave labour inheres in those who possess capital and ability. It is true that, to those who do not trace effects to their causes, there are in the economic structure of our present-day society apparent reasons for such a belief. As a student of economics I see no ground for it. It is for this reason and not from any sinister motive, that single-taxers attach no importance to the power of capital and capitalism: we know that the basis of enslavement is to be found in the expropriation of the people from the soil. It is only a stage of society where the masses have been thus expropriated that it is easy for men with capital, and ability of a questionable character, to command the services of others, at a bare subsistence wage. You will remember how Mr. Peel with his £50,000 of capital learned this lesson when he shipped 3000 persons of the working class out to the Swan River colony, and how dear old Wakefield, who recorded the story, was forced to admit that, 'Where land is cheap and all men are free, where everyone who so pleases can easily obtain a piece of land for himself, not only is labour very dear, as respects the labourer's share of the produce, but the difficulty is to get combined labour at any price.'

This inability of capital or skill to enslave labour where land is open to the workers, was clearly noted by the South African Native Affairs Commission in 1903–05 which stated:

'The natives have had access to the land on terms which have enabled them to regard work for wages as a mere supplement to their means, and that given such a population, possessing easy access to the land, it would have been extraordinary if the present situation (the difficulty of getting cheap native labour) had not followed on a very rapid growth of industrial requirements.'

These illustrations do but show the truth of the single-taxers' contention that, given free land, the capitalists together with the 'get-rich quick' gentry are powerless as exploiters.

Now, let me come to closer quarters with this theory that lumps the return of land, capital and ability under the denominator 'economic rent'. It is not sufficient to say that because the values accruing from these sources are differential, therefore, they must be treated as if they were similar in origin and character. Vitriol and water are both liquids, but to treat them on all occasions as if they were the same would bring disastrous results. I am told in the Fabian Tract 15 that 'economic rent' is the 'additional product', determined by the 'relative differences in productive efficiency of different sites and soils, capital, and forms of skill above the margin of cultivation which has gone to those exercising control over these valuable but scarce productive factors.'

I take it that you agree with this definition for you tell me that the Fabian Society could have enlisted many rich men if its constitution had not demanded the state appropriation of 'rents other than those of sites and soils'. Incidentally, may I ask if the Fabians consider the function of a man who owns sites and soils to be similar to the function of a man of marked ability? You may say, as Webb says, that both gentlemen exact all they can because of the scarcity of the thing they possess. But surely the man of ability is an asset to society, and must render a service of value in return for the wealth he appropriates, whereas the man who owns land renders no service to the community in return for the wealth which he appropriates.

We can only know a person to have ability when he is capable of performing some useful function whereby society as a whole is benefited. His ability is inseparable from his person, and through him acts as a force which leads to progress. Furthermore, the value of such ability, when appropriated by its possessor, does not subtract from the common pool of wealth, but adds to it; it is a value which is transitory and, where human intelligence is not crippled by the blight of economic privilege, is subject to the competition of the abilities of the whole community. To speak of ability being 'scarce' with the same meaning as we have in mind when we say that favourable sites and soils are scarce, is to ignore a social fact of the greatest importance: favourable sites and soils are scarce because of restrictions imposed by nature, ability, on the other hand, is, in our society, relatively scarce because of restrictions imposed by man upon man. But even though it were true that nature is niggardly in her gifts to men, upon what grounds either of justice or utility do the Fabians base their claim for the state appropriation of the values of superior ability?

Now, the owner of favourable land is a gentleman of quite another category. He, unlike the man of ability, has absolute command over the services of others, because he claims the ownership of something which, besides being essential to every activity in social life, is by nature restricted in quantity. The value of 'his' land is not temporary but permanent. The wealth he appropriates comes to him and his posterity irrespective of any service they may render and is in proportion to the necessitous demands of the community; this appropriation is therefore a subtraction from the common pool of wealth which goes to sustain a useless caste in our midst. If to this we add the power of the landowner to withhold land from use, giving rise as it does to the most damnable social anomalies, your classification of this Bill Sykes in the same category with Michael Angelo becomes somewhat startling . . .

I must confess I see no point in your last argument where you say, 'if it be true that one acre of cultivable land may, by virtue of its fertility or situation, produce ten times as much as another, it is no less true that the same acre of land in the hands of one man may produce a hundred times as much as it will produce in the hands of another, and that in the hands of certain sorts of men (higher mathematicians or Rodins for example) it will produce just nothing at all.'

Under the system of land value taxation the possessors of land, whether they be Rodins or higher mathematicians, will be forced by the pressure of the tax either to use their land in the best possible way or let to those who will . . .
Yours sincerely,
A. MacLaren.

3 October 1918.
My dear MacLaren,
You are a man of great intelligence and personal charm; and you write very well. Until you began to add a pictorial

flourish to your signature I not only thought you were a respectable man, but one of eminence, with whom I must be on my very best behaviour. Now that it dawns on me that you are only the engaging ruffian I met at Godalming I perceive that I have been the dupe of a style and of the inalienable dignity of a Scot.

I take it that the sole point of nationalising rent is that if it is left in private hands it will enable its proprietor to live at the expense of other people. If it did not, *Progress and Poverty*, would never have been written, and would have no sense. The income of the landlord is obnoxious, not because it is the rent of the land, or for any other specific quality in it, but because it is unearned income.

That being so, it is evident that to nationalise rents of soils and sites, and leave rents of capital and exceptional faculty in private hands would be to strain at a gnat and swallow a camel.

Now you may be quite right in suspecting that some of the economists [not Mill, who was an intellectually honest man and finally followed his own argument all the way to Socialism] jumped at this as a *reductio ad absurdum* of the proposal to nationalise rent. But that does not invalidate the theory any more than the single tax propaganda is invalidated by the fact that intelligent 'captains of industry' support it because they know that if successful it would only complete their mastery of the situation.

It is true that if a man gets a patch of land and makes a living out of it, no employer can tempt him into wage slavery except by offering him an equally good living as wages. For this reason the price of labour in America and Australia in the days when there was plenty of unappropriated land available for pre-emption was much higher than in England, where the land was all appropriated. But when life becomes complicated and highly civilised the organisation of production on land requires a knowledge, a business faculty, and sometimes a selfishness of which the ordinary man is incapable. If he offers the State for its nationalised land £5 an acre [representing the most he can do with it], Mr. Rockerfeller will offer £100 an acre, or [as in the City of

London, a million] and take his competitor on as a wage slave on double what the said slave would make as a petty cultivator. Try the experiment of giving, say, a common soldier, of the old professional soldier type, land and capital. You will simply ruin him in nine cases out of ten. It is like giving a soldier a ship. He can sell it and drink the proceeds; but as to navigating it, or trading with it, you might as well ask him to compose an opera.

You say, 'surely the man of ability is an asset to society, and must render a service of value in return for the wealth he appropriates.' But how if the man of ability be a thief and uses his ability to rob the community, and then to make laws legalising his sort of robbery, and punishing any sort of interference with it as a crime! After that, the devotion of ability to legalised robbery will be compulsory. It takes more ability to be a successful pirate than to command a battleship; but that does not make a pirate an asset; it rather makes an asset of the rope which hangs him. And the management of an estate requires more ability than the investment of capital and the receipt of dividends. I do both; and I know. By skinning the cultivator of the land, alive, you compel him to keep his land farmed up to the hilt, which is a service to society, as society finds when, by a Land Purchase Act, it gives the cultivator the land and discovers that he immediately lets down his farming to the level of the old income he was accustomed to when he paid a rack rent. In Russia today, peasants are asking to have the landlords back because they could at least live when they are dragooned into it; but now, left to themselves, they are starving.

The faculty of organising production is, in your own words, 'something which, besides being essential to every activity in social life, is by nature restricted in quantity'. It is far more restricted in quantity than land. You can see for yourself that it will make a penniless man a millionaire and enable him to hold as much land as he wants. His career is open to every man. How many millionaires are there? Why aren't you a millionaire? Why would I be as poor as you (if you are poor) if I had not this knack of writing plays that is almost as rare? If you were offered a thousand virgin acres to farm or organise business on, would you know how to begin? I shouldn't.

As you say, 'under the system of land values taxation the possessors of land, whether they be Rodins or higher mathematicians, will be forced by the pressure of the tax either to use their land in the best (you mean the most lucrative) possible way or to give way to those who will'. Precisely. How jolly for the Rodins and Newtons to be booted off the land with all the labourers and artisans by Rockerfeller and Co.!

Are you living in London now ? A thoct ye levvd in Glezga. I write this in Ireland, and expect to be back in London about the middle of October.
Ever,
G. Bernard Shaw.

The correspondence between MacLaren and Shaw then lapsed.

10

Protection Safeguarded

Free trade means that trade flows, like the tides, without political interference. Political control of trade and related economic matters is known as protection. The phrase 'free trade' is bandied about at the end of the twentieth century often without understanding. It is assumed that economic clubs can be formed among neighbouring nations in all corners of the globe facilitating free trade only between themselves, while the rest of mankind is excluded behind import duties. The assumption is idle, for by this exclusion free trade is effectively banished.

Protection has a timeless allure. The essence of protectionism is the belief that the welfare of a whole society can be secured by the award of economic privileges to a few at the expense of the many. It is always accompanied, as Snowden said, by 'lying propaganda'.[1]

Before describing its application in the 1930s, it is worth reviewing its melancholy history. Free trade is a piece of political archaeology. The argument between free trade and protection was settled over 200 years ago in France in 1774; covered, after a fashion, by Adam Smith's *Wealth of Nations* in 1776; demonstrated and argued from every angle by Richard Cobden, Bright and many others in the 1830s and 1840s; made the law of Britain with the repeal of the Corn Laws in 1846; applied by Jefferson in America, by Cavour in Piedmont; argued exhaustively by Bastiat; affirmed in the works of Mill and Ricardo and many other writers; rejected in the landslide election of 1906 and later argued unequivocally by Campbell-Bannerman,

---
[1] Cross, C., *Philip Snowden*, p. 245.

Asquith and Churchill. More recently it had been rejected by the people in the General Election of 1923.

Free trade was brushed aside without reasoned argument in an essay, *The End of Laissez-Faire*, by Keynes. The clouds of veneration which once gathered round Keynes, rather as they collect around a holy mountain, have dispersed at last to unmask him as a pragmatic interventionist. MacDonald opined a similar view that free trade was outdated, although his party was committed to free trade. Yet Baldwin, mindful of the electorate's rejection, advanced his concept of 'safeguarding' as something different. That was disingenuous, for plainly it was protection. He seized on the concept of safeguarding to please his party, who were firmly protectionist, and the electorate, who were firmly opposed to it.

MacLaren regarded free trade and free land as the two blades of a pair of scissors which would cut through monopolies of all sorts. Having freed production from the weight of taxation it was natural to free exchange as well. He held the view that land value taxation was the primary reform and that free trade by itself effected no appreciable change in the distribution of wealth. Protection was often justified by defending employment from the trade of the foreigners. Invariably it invoked cheap patriotism and fostered a puerile contempt for foreigners together with a sad distrust of trade. Unemployment, affirmed MacLaren, was fundamentally a fiscal problem created by heaping tax on industry and private pockets. The fact that Britain, a trading nation, was crippled in international markets was due to the fact that industry was stifled at home by monopolies and the dead-weight of taxation.

Churchill, originally a champion of free trade, became Chancellor of the Exchequer and introduced the Safeguarding of Industry Act in 1925. While Baldwin might be excused from a severe charge on account of his superficiality of mind and complete ignorance of principle, Churchill had no such defence. For in the early decades of the century he had spoken out against the injustice of tariff 'jiggles' and the corruption of political life. In 1904 he declared that Liberals believed that 'Cobden's reform would never be overturned.'[1] Yet here he was,

---

[1] Chartwell Papers 9/20/75.

just over twenty years later, presiding over the vandalism of that memory.

Churchill awarded protective tariffs to silk, artificial silk, hops, clocks, watches, musical instruments, films, motor cars and lace. There was a great deal of detail and variation in the provisions and, within three months, cutlery, scissors and razors were added. Then provisions came for gloves and gas mantles, followed by brooms and brushes and wrapping paper. It was an absurd catalogue of protectionism. Parliament assented to five conditions: the industry must be of 'substantial importance', 'exceptional' competition resulted in serious unemployment and the competition must be 'unfair', the industry must be 'reasonably efficient', and the duty must not be injurious to other British industries using the product. The selection of worthy cases was in the hands of Safeguarding Committees, whose members must not be 'materially affected'. The deliberations of these committees were so arbitrary and so open to crookery as to be ridiculous.

It was protection by the back door and there was no truth in the pretence of safeguarding anything except the producer's interest. Churchill revealed shameful dishonesty in going along with the pretence that safeguarding was different from protection. MacLaren's affection for Baldwin did not soften in the least degree his direct attack on the Safeguarding Act. It could only have been introduced, MacLaren told the Commons, by the inmates of some Babylonian asylum.

The argument that cheap goods were bad led to the absurd progression of argument that goods costing nothing at all must be the most terrible affliction to civilised man. If a foreigner offered his goods free it would be treacherous to accept them. MacLaren had been challenged on the point by the wife of a well known parson in Stoke-on-Trent. He told her to go to her husband and get him to alter the Lord's Prayer so that it was re-phrased to say: 'Do not send us this day our daily bread or You will put the bakers out of work.'

Would any student of history allege that unemployment was caused by cheap goods? Had it caused the earliest beggars to roam the roads in Tudor times? Had cheap goods caused the evident distress which obliged Elizabeth I to enact the Poor Law at the end of sixteenth century?

Under the Safeguarding Acts a person had to supply evidence that competing factories abroad worked longer hours than they did in Britain or that wages were lower. That evidence was then considered by a committee of 'unbiased' experts, who were empowered to issue a Safeguarding Order. MacLaren accused the House of involving itself with corruption, for any artificial interference with trade inevitably invited corruption. Only childish naïvety would accord public servants with the powers invested by this Act, indeed by any protectionist measure, and imagine they would exercise them in an unbiased way.

Beyond the narrow question of trade MacLaren saw the damage that protection was doing to international relations. In a debate on army estimates he said:

> There are so many things connected with this problem [military expenditure] that I feel it is utterly hopeless to attempt to deal with it on the present occasion. The real causes of militarism run much deeper than anything we have discussed tonight, and no harrowing description of the battlefield will make a man into a pacifist if he has some interest to protect. He will defend them even if the horrors of future wars are to be worse than the last. We need a common understanding how we maintain our rights as an Empire consistently with the rights of other countries. Until we have a wide discussion on the whole economic field and the relations of men, which are ruled out from the debate this evening, we cannot deal with the problems which we are attempting to discuss.[1]

MacLaren quoted freely from the speeches of Churchill, delivered as recently as 1923. But the champion of free trade was becoming a mute protectionist. Political considerations were undermining his economic understanding. In 1929 MacLaren told the House:

> We were safeguarding hollow-ware one night, needles the next night and buttons the night after; and really one

---
[1] Hansard, col. 970 7:3:27.

wondered whether one was in the House of Commons or in Selfridge's bargain basement. This is the pass to which British politics has come – that we have to turn this House of Commons into a veritable assessment room and analyse the various values of articles from ladies' stockings to corsets. (Laughter). Why do men laugh at this sort of thing? Because it is ridiculous. You cannot laugh at that which is true; you can only laugh at that which is utterly ridiculous.[1]

A case in point; the Film Bill sought to protect British film makers abroad. Yet German films were far superior in 1927 and protection was not going to conjure up the artistic skills for making outstanding films. MacLaren challenged the Opposition to quote one country which enjoyed protection without slums, poverty and corruption. They suggested Australia was such an example, though MacLaren was not impressed. 'For corruption,' he replied, 'for double dealing between so-called trade union leaders and men of this party and the other party, for joint meetings behind tariff walls, dividing the spoils and making the consumer pay, there is no country in Europe that can equal Australia.'[2]

It was the methods of protecting rural landowners under the misconceived guise of protecting British agriculture which especially drew MacLaren's attention, or rather fire. Since the subsidies and relief heaped on agriculture were claimed at the end of the lease by the landowner, the tenant farmer was no better off as a result of being awarded the subsidies claimed in his name. In economic analysis the situation of the tenant is that of every farmer. Those who own the freehold of their property differ only in that they amalgamate the interests of tenant farmer and freehold landowner in one person.

The Corn Laws were repealed in 1846, lifting protection from agriculture. But the hind teeth of landlordism lingered in the Lords and on the backbenches of the Commons. They could afford to wait until this insane experiment in free trade would falter and protection could be welcomed back.

---
[1] Ibid., cols 613–4 8:7:29.
[2] Ibid., 4:3:30.

In 1896 rates were abolished on agricultural land and the effect of relieving the burden of £1.3 million was, in the words of Lloyd George, to drive the taxpayer 'into the landlords' leech-pond.' Between 1917 and 1921 the Corn Production Act gave farmers a guaranteed price for their wheat. Both measures gave rise to a land rush even though agriculture was said to be on its knees. Many tenants had been presented with the choice of buying the freehold of their holdings. The repeal of the Corn Production Act left these buyers in the lurch with high borrowings; just another example of how Parliament can intend one thing and, because of the lack of economic insight of its members, achieve something quite different. In 1923 the Government enacted relief in the form of the Agricultural Credits Act. There was a further relief of rates in 1923 on agricultural buildings and the complete de-rating in 1929. MacLaren argued that these four Acts protected landlords, rather than agriculture.

He used the same argument against measures to assist in the purchase of smallholdings, to assist the costs of land drainage, canal widening, sugar beet production, rural road building, agricultural education, marketing agricultural produce, relaxation of death duties, taxation under Schedule B and the tithe.

When challenged on the floor of the House as to whether the Labour Government had not taken a hand in the sugar beet legislation, MacLaren minded not which party had been involved; it was a poor measure. He did not suffer that seemingly incurable blindness of the party. Not only was the landowner saved the expense, by one device or another, but he was the beneficiary of expenditure. It would have been an injustice if they had even paid taxes.

MacLaren deplored the subventions given in 1925 ostensibly to relieve the rates.

> Last week they made great concessions to the very monopoly [landlordism] which is crippling the mining industry and ... they tell us that this crash may come in May [and] can be averted if we will all be good boys, join hands, sing some Christian hymns and then we shall all be happy ever after. Such an appeal is not only childish, but

futile. It is playing with the confidence of the distressed public outside. You cannot solve this problem of the mines until you challenge the ownership of the raw materials of the earth which are now in private hands, until you do something to encourage the industry by removing the enormous burden of rates which fall upon mining development in this country, until you relieve the pressure of rates and taxes ... Whether a mine has a good running or a bad running the first charge is the royalties, which are a subsidy to the landlords from beginning to end. When we are told there are malingerers who take the dole, malingerers who get round various Acts of Parliament, who sponge on the State, I wonder what the landowners of England are thinking about. They do not require to sponge or go before the unemployment committee. They can go to their hunt, they can go to Monte Carlo, they can go to Heaven or the other place. Their royalties are secured, even by subsidy, in their absence.[1]

MacLaren went on to advocate some form of national control, even nationalisation. He was not in favour, however, of nationalisation with no alteration of taxation.

At the Second Reading of the Coal Mines Bill 1926, MacLaren said:

You find the proposition coming across the floor of the House that there is no way out of the impasse into which the mining industry has got, except by longer hours or a reduction of wages ... Why is it that this conservative, stupid, block-headed system maintains itself in British industry? You want to economise, because you are in competition with other nations and, immediately, you fly at what you seem to think the weakest link in the defence, namely, wages of the worker, instead of throwing into wages all you can in order to encourage the workers to produce the most they can and put enthusiasm into their labour.

---

[1] Ibid., cols 797–8 10:12:25.

The other day I went into a hotel in my own Division, and I saw a good number of fellows enjoying a good dinner. I asked: 'Who are these chaps?' The reply was: 'They are members of a football team.' I said: 'You are feeding them well,' to which I got the reply: 'Yes, we feed them well, pay them well, train them well and house them well.' I said: 'How strange! You do that when you want to win a football cup, but when you want to work in the mines you dock the wages, house them badly, and feed them badly.' It seemed ironical ... The housing condition in the Potteries that I represent in this House is unfit for brute beasts, and I have to go back and to say to these miners: 'Under the new conditions, you will have to accept £1 19s 5d in wages, and an extended hour on your day.' We have had our food today. We have clean bodies and we have home accommodation. It is hard indeed for us to get into the psychology of men living under these rotten conditions, and to go back to these men and tell them that the best thing that this House of Commons, that boasts of being the Mother of Parliaments, the best thing that 600 men of general intelligence and capacity for understanding legal enactments can offer them is that the finest adjustment in the economic production of coal is not the cutting down of overhead charges, nor the re-organisation of the mines, but that they shall work for less wages and longer hours.[1]

In July 1929 Lord Beaverbroook launched his concept of 'Empire Free Trade', forming an alliance with Lord Rothermere on the issue. S.W. Alexander, a journalist and free trader, explained why Beaverbrook proclaimed this policy so fervently. It was good commercial sense. Beaverbrook advocated protection to earn advertising from the firms favoured by the wives of farmers and other protected folk. When a United Empire party candidate beat a Conservative, Baldwin attacked the two press chiefs. He accused them of wanting power without responsibility and, borrowing a phrase from his cousin Rudyard Kipling, described this as 'the prerogative of the harlot throughout the ages.' The 'United Empire' sideshow soon folded.

---

[1] Ibid., cols 949–52 28:6:26.

MacDonald's Minister of Unemployment, Jimmy Thomas, was aided in Cabinet by an ambitious adventurer called Mosley – both were protectionist thinkers. Mosley had been a Conservative Member who felt the time was right for experimenting in state intervention in the economy. Lloyd George was being advised by Keynes, who advocated the use of borrowed funds to finance public works. This policy seemed a lot more exciting than the government's non-interventionist one. Snowden was resolutely set against this intervention, insisting with Thomas that spending should be 'economically sound'.[1] Mosley and Lansbury drew up the Mosley Memorandum, as it came to be called. It provided for 750,000 extra jobs at a cost of £10 million per annum. People were to be pensioned off at sixty and the school leaving age was to be raised. Import boards were also part of this economically distasteful cocktail.

MacDonald was impressed by Mosley, whom he regarded as an aristocrat – MacDonald preferred them to socialists. Mosley's first wife, Cynthia, was the daughter of Lord Curzon, a paragon of snobbery. Cynthia followed her husband devotedly into the Labour Party. In 1929 she became Labour member for a neighbouring constituency in Stoke. MacLaren was struck by her candour and friendship. He pitied her for being neglected by her husband in favour of his wild political schemes and philandering. He saw her being pushed into hopelessness which deprived her of the will to survive an attack of peritonitis. Mosley allowed the disagreement with Snowden and Thomas to become a battle within the Labour Party, but in May 1930 Mosley resigned to form his New Party, which failed spectacularly.

In June 1930 MacDonald told the Commons that he had invited the Conservatives and the Liberals to 'a pooling of ideas'. Lloyd George accepted with alacrity but the Conservatives were unable to drop their protectionism as a pre-condition. In March 1931 Keynes advanced his demands in a standard protectionist way, although he was able to disguise their nature by arguing only for a temporary tariff sufficient, he pretended, to boost home employment and revenue. So devious was the argument that it gave rise to a typical defence of Keynes; that what was

---

[1] Grigg, P.J., *Prejudice and Judgement*, p. 242.

being done by the Government was not quite what he had advised. If that is to be sustained it follows that Keynes was naive in imagining that protection could be picked up and set down like a child's toy. It could not be applied and taken off at will.

MacLaren expressed his general philosophy in 1931 thus:

> I wish to protest that I have never known anything more fatuous than the idea that a bureaucracy can come and collect money from individuals' pockets and spend it far better than can the individuals themselves. It arises from the fallacious idea that it is the function of the State to bring about something like equality in the distribution of wealth. Instead of removing the injustices which give rise to the maldistribution of wealth, it has become a new idea that we must have a very efficient form of bureaucracy in Whitehall, who, in their day and generation, will go about collecting money from those who have it, and spend it with greater wisdom among the poor . . . act in such a way as to remove privilege and monopoly, and allow the wealth produced by labour to diffuse itself through society, and not be congealed by privileges and vested interests, then you will not require to have a highly-paid bureaucracy acting like balancing balls on a steam engine, and doing in an artificial way that which would have been done in a natural way if you had originally removed the powers of the vested interests.[1]

On assuming office as Chancellor of the Exchequer in 1929, Snowden told the House of Commons that there would be no further safeguarding duties and that the existing ones would be allowed to expire. Yet within three years the country panicked and protection was reintroduced. But, as usual, it provided no solution.

In September 1935 MacLaren joined with Lansbury in a document circulated among Members of Parliament warning that protection was at the root of the troubles in Europe. They

---
[1] Hansard cols 749–50 2:10:31.

traced the difficulties from the acceptance at Versailles of the Wilsonian doctrine of the right of self-determination. The implementation of that doctrine was left to the League of Nations. The difficulty was to fix geographical boundaries which were deemed sufficient for defence and for economic protection. Czechoslovakia was a good example. It contained large pockets of Germans and Poles, who were claiming the right to self determination. The word 'boundary' meant 'custom union' to the continental mind. Although it seemed the struggle was political and racial, plebiscites to determine the boundaries of states were used to further tariff barriers. This 'disintegrated state', as MacLaren termed it, of middle-Europe led to quarrels between small nations and to war between the larger ones. They called upon European statesmen to put in place the economic foundation for the League of Nations.

MacLaren and Lansbury wrote a paper with Richard Stokes in October 1938. It concentrated on the economic significance of the expansion of Germany. They were possessed of every raw material needed for an assault on world industrial markets. While the British government was pursuing a policy to raise prices by use of quotas, subsidies and tariffs, Germany was pursuing an opposite policy. Britain must abandon protection and cut the taxes falling upon production – that is all taxation and rates – in order to reduce prices. They discountenanced a cut in wage levels.

MacLaren argued persistently for free trade. But he never pretended that it was a magic wand which could be waved at every problem. It did not concern the distribution of wealth, nor did it cause unemployment, inflation or poverty. He saw it as a secondary issue, which could save governments rushing down endless blind alleys. As Churchill had stated in 1909, it was essential to enjoy land value taxation and free trade together.

11

The Land Question

On assuming office in June 1929, MacDonald declared: 'A Chancellor of the Exchequer who takes taxes off this country deserves the gratitude of the country; a Labour Chancellor will do this.' In the King's speech a coalition between the parties was also hinted at.

Philip Snowden, the Chancellor, inherited a weak financial position from Churchill, who had only achieved a balanced Budget by some creative accounting during prosperous years. His last Budget in 1929 yielded a deficit of £14 million. Snowden's first act was to insist that Britain's share of the reparations exacted from Germany should be higher than those agreed by the Young Committee. He stuck out for a figure some £1 million per annum higher than recommended by that body. He returned to London something of a hero, cutting a more effective and direct character than MacDonald.

The stock market crash in New York had set off the worst international depression of the twentieth century which endured until 1932. Snowden increased the bank rate by 1 per cent and appointed the Macmillan Committee to look into the financial system. His first domestic problem was that the Unemployment Fund, designed to be self-financing from 'contributions' deducted from employers and employees, was overdrawn. In keeping with his integrity, he decided to meet the deficit out of taxation, including the cost in his estimate of increased expenditure of £19 million per annum.

The number of unemployed had reached two million by July 1930 and within six months it had increased by a further half a million. This overshadowed events and brought with it fear, doubt and sentimental politics. There was a widespread call for resort to protection, but Snowden stood firm for free trade. MacLaren eagerly awaited the Budget in 1930.

Snowden had entered Parliament in 1906, having been one of the founding fathers of the Labour parliamentary party. Initially he had been in favour of land nationalisation. A measure which had all the hallmarks of socialism: wildly impractical, superficially emotional and as injurious to the people as it was beneficial to landowners. But Snowden later realised that, far from compensating landowners for their appropriation, government should tax them into extinction.

On 24 May 1919 he had told a London audience: 'Until they abolished landlordism root and branch, every other attempt at reform was building upon sands. Every reform not based on common ownership of land was simply subsidising landlordism. Every social reform increased the economic rent of land. Therefore, unless they were going to waste their efforts by tinkering with social questions as in the past, they must concentrate upon this fundamental question, to secure the land for the people.'

The outgoing Tory administration had accumulated a debt of £36 million in respect of sums lent to the Unemployment Insurance Fund which Lloyd George had opened in 1911. Annual expenditure on unemployment rose from £47 million in 1929 to about £92 million in 1931. During 1930 the government was borrowing £1 million a month. Indeed, the world was being ravaged, as Churchill observed, by 'the worst economic blizzard ever known'. Snowden could not afford to do without revenue of any description and left intact various 'safeguarding' duties which Churchill had imposed in 1925, raising £10 million a year. He cut unemployment pay by 10 per cent and transferred its payment to the Public Assistance Committees of local authorities who were obliged to operate a strict 'means test' to ascertain the financial circumstances of the applicant. His cautious increases and moderation on income and surtax angered his more militant members. Neither did Snowden include any measure for land taxation; indeed, he took a swipe at the land-taxers. 'Some of my land-tax friends,' he told the Commons, 'are difficult people to please. They are like people with one idea; they think there is nothing else of the least importance. But there are other questions. We have a terribly overcrowded parliamentary programme.'

MacLaren could not hide his disappointment. He told the *Manchester Guardian*: 'Our optimism has been shaken. His speech has left the single-taxer speechless. We can neither praise nor damn him. He has thrown us into a comatose condition, and only vain hope keeps us alive for another year.' Land value taxation was not just an *idée fixe* to MacLaren; it was the basic reform.

In 1930 MacLaren served on the Select Committee which examined the project proposed by the London County Council to bridge the Thames at Charing Cross. The cost was fixed at £14.6 million. A figure which compared unfavourably with the cost of the Sydney harbour bridge [£9.5 million] and a two and a half mile long bridge in Denmark [less than £2 million]. The Committee rejected the plan on the grounds that economy was the watchword at the time. What MacLaren found particularly interesting was the fact that the cost included a figure of £11.1 million to be paid as compensation to the riparian landowners, including Jesus College, Oxford and the Ecclesiastical Commissioners. Though this expense was necessary to get the bridge built it would be more than offset by the rise in land values when the bridge was completed. MacLaren enquired of the valuer, who would pocket this increment? The question neither received nor needed an answer; MacLaren had drawn attention to the real situation. That a democratic people should allow the private appropriation of communally created land value was, to him, quite extraordinary.

At Westminster the Conservatives and the Liberals were in disunion. Both their leaders, Baldwin and Lloyd George, were clinging to power. MacDonald was becoming deranged and Snowden fell ill at the end of 1930. A Council of State composed of representatives of each party was formed to solve the increasing indebtedness.

Throughout the early months of 1931 there was growing disquiet in the City, the Bank of England becoming alarmed at the budgetary deficit. In February, Snowden took the House of Commons into his confidence. He told members, suddenly, quietly and with precise articulation, that the estimate of the annual deficit to 31 March 1932 was projected to be of the order of £50 million, and he appointed a committee headed by Sir George May to look into the deficit.

He had kept control of policy in relation to the Budget from his sick bed and insisted on hobbling into the House to present it. He feared to give way now would hand national finances on a plate into the rather indecisive hand of MacDonald.

Churchill had earlier drawn the attention of the House to MacDonald's failure to respond to the crisis. He recalled that: '... when I was a child being taken to the celebrated Barnam's Circus ... the exhibit which I most desired to see the one described as the 'Boneless Wonder'. My parents judged that the spectacle would have been too revolting to my youthful eyes, and I have waited fifty years to see the Boneless Wonder sitting on the Treasury Bench.'

Snowden had promised a Land Valuation Bill. It appeared in July 1930 and was included in the Finance Bill 1931. In the King's Speech of October 1930 MacLaren was gladdened by the statement that a 'Bill for securing to the people its share in the site value of land'.

The Budget of 1931 was a cautious one. The only addition to taxation was 2d a gallon on petrol and it was uncertain whether the projected deficit was covered. But to MacLaren it was a memorable Budget because it introduced land value taxation. This was assessed at 1d on the capital, or selling price, of land. In his speech the Chancellor said: 'When we have carried this measure [on land value taxation] ... we shall look back upon th[is] budget as a landmark on the road of social and economic progress, and as one further stage towards the emancipation of the people from the tyranny and the injustice of private land monopoly.'[1]

At the Third Reading, Snowden spoke especially of the land taxes.

> The principle underlying the Bill, is to assert the right of the community to the ownership of land. I have never made

---
[1] Mallet, B., *British Budgets 1921–33*, p. 330.

any question about that, nor that right should be expressed in the form of a rent paid by the occupier, or rather the owner of land, to the community. As I said, just now, this is only the first step in the reform of our land system. The effect of that system, is to place a burden on industry of hundreds of million a year. It has crowded our people into pestilential slums, and it has driven hundreds of thousands of people from the land, to the towns, to compete with the town workers, with the result that wages have been depressed and unemployment has increased ... I submit this Bill to the House of Commons with the satisfaction that I believe we have begun a far reaching reform which some day will liberate the land for the people and abolish forces and tyranny under which the people of this country have suffered.

Snowden had favoured the nationalisation of land and voiced this opinion quite openly during the 1909 Budget controversy. He had modified his view since, largely because of the efforts of the persuasion of the land-taxers. Leaving aside the means to pay for such a gigantic programme of nationalisation, MacLaren argued that, as the private ownership of land value was an injustice, there was no argument for compensating landowners, if their usurpations were terminated by the State.

In fact Snowden was keenly aware of how Lloyd George had endeavoured to tax increment value in 1909 and how he had failed dismally. All that remained was a general unease and an efficient Valuation Department of the Inland Revenue. Snowden chose to tax an annual value and resisted the popular concept of capital values.

In order to make the Valuation Bill qualify as a Budget measure, a tax of a penny in the pound was imposed. 'Once we got the valuation,' explained Snowden, 'it would be for a future government to decide what the tax should be.'[1] There were exemptions, however, despite Lloyd George's advice against allowing 'exemptions, trickeries, reductions and limitations.' But, having pledged his full support, Lloyd-George then altered

---
[1] Snowden, P., *Autobiography*, vol. 2, p. 910.

the Liberal position, whereby they accepted a reduction of the value of land to no more than four times the annual value for Schedule A of Income Tax. Snowden, however, acceded to exemptions for land used for statutory purposes, by local authorities, church land and relief for agricultural land. MacLaren opposed these exemptions and reliefs. But the schemes of Lloyd George held no charm for the Chancellor. He had produced a Bill containing a valuation of most land. The work done on the valuation of 1909 could be used, although in most cases it would need to be updated.

Lloyd George congratulated MacLaren, after he had finished speaking on the Finance Bill in the Committee of Ways and Means. 'This is my honourable friend's happy day,' he told the Commons. 'When these occasions arise, too often there is a feeling of disillusionment, but I am glad to find in the case of my honourable friend, the Member for Burslem, he is very happy. I congratulate him on seeing the coming accomplishment of a great many years of hard work in converting public opinion to the acceptance of this idea, the taxation of land values.'[1]

Indeed MacLaren was, at last, in sight of the summit to which he had been aiming for the past nineteen years. He always disdained being called a politician, preferring to be called a single-taxer. That rather inelegant appellation conveyed his purpose more directly.

MacLaren believed that the art of politics, was the readiness to accept a better idea, and then to bring that idea into the administrative operations of government. No-one put forward an idea to challenge the one in which he believed though he was quite ready, even during the last days of his life, to debate the matter with anyone.

In his speech to the Ways and Means Committee, he brushed aside the idea that individuals create the value of land. Sir William Morris was reckoned to have created land value at Oxford, and the Cadbury family at Bournville. If that was true, suggested MacLaren, let them prove their miraculous powers in the Sahara desert, where there was no communal demand. He

---

[1] Hansard, col. 432, 6:5:31.

quoted from a speech delivered in 1913 by Lloyd George to illustrate the injustice of the rates. 'You can imagine for a moment that I am an assessor,' [No doubt the town would quake at that] 'operating under the modern rating system and that when I go outside Leeds, to the moors, I come across the owner of the moors. I say to him "What are you doing with this land?" "Oh," he says, "I am just holding it for so many years' purchase, because the Leeds Corporation want it for a reservoir for the Corporation". And I, as assessor, say: "Give me your hand. I suppose you want that money for that land because it is disturbing your pheasants."

Hon. Members: Grouse!

Mr. MacLaren: Oh, grouse is it. You see I am not accustomed to shooting. Make it 'disturbing your pheasants' or 'your grouse' whichever you like. I would rather that members paid attention to the story than to the details. The assessor was saying:

"Such men as you make the country rich." Going down the road I meet a certain manufacturer in the town who has improved his factory. He has made it more spacious and comfortable for the workers. I go along and say: "Have you improved this factory?" – That was before the Derating Act! – When he says he has, I make a new valuation and levy an increased rate on the man because he has improved his factory. Then I meet a man who has put a bathroom into his house. I say: "Have you put a bathroom in your house?" "Yes," he replies. "Well, I say, there is another couple of pounds on your rates for daring to do so. Do not let me hear of you doing it again!" Then I go down to the slums, and when I meet the owner of the slums I say to him: "Have you improved your property since I was here five years ago?" He says: "No, Sir." So I say: "Well done, thou good and faithful servant. Go down to the rating office and ask them to reduce your rates 12s 6d in the £." ' The right honourable member for Carnavon Boroughs, after giving his parable, said: 'Do you think I am caricaturing? That is the rating system'.[1]

There had been complaints on the other side of the House of the expenses involved in the valuation of land. Though

---
[1] Ibid., col. 424–5, 6:5:31.

MacLaren was prepared to take a landowner's word in the place of a State valuation provided that the estimate was used at sale or for probate. The valuation would be costly. It was to be a new Domesday Book. The initial cost would be high but the continuing costs of maintaining it would be negligible. He congratulated the Chancellor for making the valuation open to public inspection pointing out that this had not been done in 1909. He concluded by noting, sadly, that Churchill was absent and would miss being reminded of the speech which he made at Drury Lane Theatre in April 1907. 'The right honourable gentleman [Churchill] is a master of language, of simile, and of dextrous, flashing, brilliant eloquence. He knows much more than I do the value and weight of words . . .'[1]

Later, in Committee, the Tories relied on Edward Majoribanks to make their attack on the Finance Bill. He approached MacLaren to make arrangements to inspect the material MacLaren intended to use in the debate. MacLaren allowed him unconditional access to his locker and declined to avail himself of a reciprocal offer; he knew the case so well that he could predict the arguments his opponent would use. MacLaren threw back the Tory charge that Labour were appropriating private property like the Bolsheviks. The land was the common property of mankind and the Tories, like the Bolsheviks, were appropriating it for certain individuals. The Commons was not used to debating the philosophy of property outside the tribal slogans of class.

Edward Cadogan was particularly concerned to corner this radical thinker. An interjection of his in the debate was typical:

'Mr. MacLaren: True, the lawyers have made out that, in practice, land is private property.

Mr. Cadogan: It belongs to the King.

Mr. MacLaren: Yes, it belongs to the King, but he does not collect the rent.

Mr. Cadogan: What a quibble!'

Later Cadogan asked him to define what he meant by the word property, and to show how land differed from other sorts of property. MacLaren delighted in nothing as much as answering that sort of basic question.

---

[1] Ibid., col. 431, 6:5:31.

First of all my property claim is based on the fact that I produced the thing by my own labour, or that I have exchanged something that I have produced for the thing that I am now claiming, or that it has been bequeathed me by someone who either produced it by their own labour or exchanged it for something they produced, the cardinal, rock bottom principle being that property cannot be established unless there is a title deed of labour establishing it. The distinguishing thing between other forms of property and land is this, that while other things which are deemed to be property have labour added to them to establish a property claim in proportion to the labour expended upon them, land was never produced by any man.[1]

The Tories argued that the state was going to penalise small shopkeepers by taxing them. Did a landlord ever hold his hand because the small man had got behind with his rental? No sooner was there a proposal to tax land, than there was an avalanche of post, claiming exemptions, which had never been addressed to, or considered by, a private landlord. But the debate was interesting because it included a reasoned reply from the Tory benches. What had been the aggressive silence and the accompanying disdain was now to be expressed as an argument. Majoribanks acknowledged MacLaren's sincerity but likened him to a religious figure who imagined the earth was flat or who believed that the saviours of the world were two Cromwellian soldiers. He made a weak speech and to precis his points lends them a cogency which they never had. Land was no different from all other forms of property, though this is patent nonsense. To attack this form of property was to attack friendly societies, trade unions and educational institutions. The Tories often identify themselves with the small farmer, the small shopkeeper and the destitute beggar and never with the prosperous, fat, bewhiskered folk who funded their party. Majoribanks referred to the experience of a land tax in America. Here, he noted that the tax was passed on by the landlord.

---

[1] Ibid., col. 916, 9:6:31.

He objected to the expense of collecting the tax. This point may have counted for something in a parliamentary debate, in which the speaker desired to obfuscate, rather than to argue principles. He objected to the proposed land taxes 'because these taxes can only work if they are flagrantly unjust.' What he meant by these words is unclear. Finally, like a good Tory, he wrapped himself in patriotic fervour. 'American influence,' he stated, 'has not been such a healthy influence upon the life of this country. It has invaded our beautiful language, it has corrupted our music, it has scarred our great capital city with its hideous architecture, and now it is not really appropriate that we should go back for our economic salvation to an American economist who was profoundly ignorant of the history of his own times and whose philosophy is wholly inappropriate to our own.'[1]

In June the Gregory Commission delivered its report on the Unemployment Fund and recommended a reduction of 30 per cent in benefits and their limitation to 26 weeks. The failure of the government to deal with the report alarmed the City. The Reparations demanded from Germany between 1924–31 were over £1 billion. For the first four years Germany met their liability from foreign investments and other resources. But in the first six months of 1930 Germany had to borrow a third of the sums due and in the first half of the following year she could no longer pay. There was an immediate loss of credit and withdrawals of £150 million short term deposits. In May the Credit Anstalt Bank, responsible for two thirds of the Austrian bank deposits, closed its doors in Vienna, precipitating the failures of the Darmstadt and Dresden Banks in Germany. The Bank of England advanced £4 million to Austria in June But after German reparations of £50 million were frozen, pressure was immediately placed on sterling. The Bank of England suffered losses of gold reserves amounting to £33 million in two weeks.

Distrust sparked a political reaction. There was a rush to protection. It was as if the drunk was seeking salvation in whisky. Churchill, hitherto a solid Free Trader, joined with the TUC, much of the Liberal Party and Keynes in embracing this popular panacea.

---

[1] Ibid., col. 929–30, 9:6:31.

In the midst of this confusion Snowden published the Macmillan Report on banking in July, which rejected the option of devaluation out of hand. The Report was notable for the Minority Report signed by Keynes, McKenna, Ernest Bevin and others, who were 'advocating the whole paraphernalia of public works plus tariffs or devaluation, according to the varying taste of the signatories.'[1] The danger with Keynes was not in what he said. It was that people believed him. But Snowden did not and he refused to be drawn on the financial crisis.

During the debate on the land valuation clauses, the Labour benches gradually became aware that the Tories had soon run out of their favourite ammunition and persiflage. 'We realised,' recounted MacLaren many years later, 'that the Tories were beaten to a frazzle. After the Committee of Ways and Means debate I left the chamber with Snowden. He was delighted with the turn of events.' The Bill had gone through with only one minor change regarding Schedule A of the Income tax regime. He recalled that he had never heard the Tories so quiet in debate. I said: "I was convinced they would have a trick up their sleeves." '

---

[1] Grigg, J.P., *Prejudice and Judgement*, p. 253.

12

Coalition and Confusion

In July 1931 there were 2.8 million unemployed living off the State. The government arranged loans of foreign exchange worth about £50 million in Paris and New York. The May Committee reported in 300 pages at the end of July. They predicted that the budget deficit for the year 1931/32 would exceed £120 million and recommended savings of £96 million in social expenditure, notably in a 20 per cent cut in unemployment pay, which would save £66 million, and £24 million in increased taxes.

Publication of the May Committee report further worried the City. There was a run on gold, silver and foreign exchanges. Baldwin and Neville Chamberlain offered partnership between the parties in order to calm fears.

Before the politicians met, the Treasury projected the deficit in the following year would rise to £170 million. The bankers in London told MacDonald that '[t]he cause of the trouble was not financial, but political, and lay in the complete want of confidence in HMG existing among foreigners.'[1] They demanded that the Budget must be balanced by a reduction in expenditure.

MacDonald briefed the opposition leaders in August 1931. The Cabinet met on 24 August and, after much suspense, agreed to cut unemployment pay by only 10 per cent, a hard step for the Socialists. Another proposal to impose a 10 per cent revenue tariff was met by Snowden threatening to resign. But the cut in the unemployment dole was insufficient for the

---
[1] Fielding, A., *Neville Chamberlain*, p. 191.

bankers of New York and Paris, who were making loans available to Britain.

When the Cabinet met MacDonald told them nothing of what was afoot. However, that same day MacDonald went to see the king, who agreed to meet him the next day with Stanley Baldwin and Sir Herbert Samuel. 'Taking all these things together,' observed Snowden, 'I think they give grounds for the suspicion expressed by Mr. Henderson and other Labour Ministers, that Mr. MacDonald had deliberately planned the scheme of a national government, which would at the same time enable him to retain the position of Prime Minister and associate with political colleagues with whom he was more in sympathy, than he had ever been with his [own] political colleagues.'[1]

The National Government was described not as a coalition but rather as a co-operation between friends. It was formed of the Socialists, under MacDonald, the Conservatives and the Liberals and intended to deal only with the financial emergency. MacLaren remained profoundly unimpressed by the direness of the emergency, the accompanying climate of anxiety and the formation and address of the government. To him it was more like a pantomime than reality. Churchill, who had been a leading minister of Baldwin's government and who, more recently, had resigned from the Conservative shadow cabinet over disagreement on Indian policy in 1930, was also against the National Government. On 8 September he called for an election in order to strengthen the government and to introduce protection.

On the day after it was formed, MacDonald visited Snowden, who recorded: 'I remarked to him that he would find himself very popular in strange quarters. He replied, gleefully rubbing his hands: "Yes, tomorrow every Duchess in London will be wanting to kiss me." '[2] The Cabinet consisted of ten ministers, four Labour, four Conservatives and two Liberals. Fresh loans of £40 million were raised in both Paris and New York.

What was also surprising was to see Lloyd George champion-

---
[1] Snowden, P., *Autobiography*, vol. 2, p. 954.
[2] Ibid., p. 957.

ing free trade, though he had never done so before. The contrary attitudes of both men echo a statement by Asquith in 1908: 'Lloyd George had no principles and Churchill no convictions.'[1] Indeed it was as sad to see Churchill reject a principle which he so manfully upheld from the beginning of his parliamentary life as it was to see Lloyd George lend his tactical support to a principle of a grandeur far above political party manoeuvring. MacLaren had already seen Churchill abandon his zeal for the taxation of land values and he was too disappointed by that to be much saddened by Churchill's final abandonment of free trade. It had been coming ever since the First War.

The Liberals were also split on the question. MacDonald was not committed to either camp and was in favour of an election in which both sides could express their views. He was aptly described by A.J.P. Taylor as 'the master of imprecision.' He asked the electorate for a 'doctor's mandate' by which he meant a blank cheque to cure the ills of politics. He pretended that the emergency was greater than the fiscal question.

Snowden presented an Emergency Budget on 10 September. The financial measures agreed by Parliament were identical to those previously accepted by the Labour Cabinet – economies of £70 million – except they agreed in addition to impose £81 million in new taxation. The cuts in expenditure had entailed a reduction in earnings of 10 per cent. A devastating blow was dealt to public confidence when naval personnel went out on strike – that is to say, mutinied – at Invergordon on 15 September. The run on the pound continued until 19 September and only abated when the pound sterling was taken off the Gold Standard. Gone was one of the self-correcting mechanisms of the economy. It was an essential prelude to State planning. A.J.P. Taylor wittily observed that though the standard in planning was Utopia, the reality remained a dismal failure in so many fields.

MacLaren was not alone in suspecting that the financial crises had been used to exaggerate the situation. *The Daily Herald*, which continued to support the Labour Party, dubbed the whole episode as a 'bankers' ramp'.

---

[1] R. Churchill, *Winston Churchill*, vol. ii, p. 247.

On 27 October there was a General Election. It was a bitter election campaign. MacLaren's principal opponent was William Allen KC, a National candidate and a most solemn guardian of the 'national interest'. He was a protectionist. Like a creature emerging from the slimy depths of a dark pond, he pretended that protectionism was created precisely for such a grave hour. Being an eminent lawyer, he was skilled in speaking about everything without particularising anything. He had sat in Parliament from 1892–1921 and opened by suggesting that MacLaren should declare himself an independent. MacLaren replied that he had considered becoming a Tory but, after reading the speeches of their leaders, felt 'most heartfelt sympathy to the poor reporters who have to write up such tripe night after night ... I would not be found dead among the National Government. If I go back to the House of Commons and find more Ramsay MacDonalds there, I am going to have it out. I am not anymore going to keep my lips sealed, as I have done these last seven years.'

Much of the campaign was taken up with the issue of protectionism. Snowden and MacDonald turned on the Labour Party for its unwillingness to accept cuts in expenditure. In his election address MacLaren wrote: 'Ineptitude and pseudo-patriotism have forced upon us a general election. A unique set of oddments have formed themselves into a National Government. They contain within their circle men whom you know are utterly incapable of solving the merest secondary national problem. Now they ask you, the Electors, to return them to power, not on the basis of economic principles, but on non-committal pledges and "a free hand" ... Since the War we have witnessed the hapless blundering statesmen in every country. The iniquities of the Versailles Treaty have been swift in their retribution. Inhuman and impossible terms were imposed upon the vanquished and we have seen as time advances how the victors have had to raise loans to help the vanquished pay the tribute ... America and France behind tariff walls demanded payments of indemnities and debts. They refused to take commodities and would only accept gold. By the beginning of September [1931] these two controlled between them, three fourths of the world's gold supply and were still demanding more ... Great Britain, who had wiped out £44 million of War debt due to her by France, and who pays to America £100,000 per day in respect of War debts, had to raise loans in these countries amounting to £130 million ... In almost every home unemployment is to be found. Our people are being asked to suffer the indignities of poverty and unemployment as a result of the misdirections, and in some cases the personal motives, of those who claim to be our statesmen.' MacLaren pointed out, that in the US, the most highly protected nation on earth, unemployment ran to 12 million. *The Manchester Guardian* called it: 'the most fraudulent campaign of modern times.'

MacLaren lost his seat by 2,399 votes. The dangers were so great, it was widely felt, that a National Government was the only answer. MacLaren thought more simply that the vested interests did not trust Labour with sole control of the State.

In 1929 Labour had held 289 seats but after the Election in 1931 they held only 46. The Labour Party, now led by Lansbury, had been knocked senseless. Snowden was in no doubt as to the cause of the debacle. 'I have read the Election programme of the Labour Party,' he said in a radio broadcast, 'It is the most impracticable fantasy ever put before the electors. This is not socialism. It is Bolvsehism run mad.' The Liberals held only 33 seats. Snowden, who had been the major supporter a free trade, went to the Lords as Lord Privy Seal and the Chancellorship fell to Neville Chamberlain.

The election result reflected an electorate voting from fear which had spread sufficiently for MacDonald to be able to pose as a national saviour; in fact he was really the crafty and cowardly undertaker of the nation's liberties. History was to show that the British people had chosen unwisely.

Absence from the House of Commons gave MacLaren pause to paint and teach. He started the Land Values Bureau near Trafalgar Square and gave classes there on Wednesday evenings and Sunday afternoons. The Marquis of Tavistock and Father Mcnabb, a Catholic monk and close friend, also spoke. Vincent Mcnabb was a scholar of Aquinas and a fundamental thinker with the zeal of Savanrola. G.K. Chesterton described him as 'one of the outstanding personalities of my generation.'

Within a month of the election Chamberlain had proposed the repeal of the land valuation provisions even though the National Government had been formed on the understanding that the 1931 Budget would remain in force. Snowden wanted to resign over the issue but was persuaded to stay by a tearful MacDonald, who recounted how much they had gone through together. Chamberlain explained that he was under pressure from his Party in the Commons to repeal the 1931 valuation procedures. It was necessary, in order to continue the expense of valuation, to submit a Vote on the Estimates but his members would not assent to the measure. So the valuation was suspended. The Tories wanted repeal, so that they could sleep soundly at night, instead of being haunted by the spectre of an impassioned radical like Andrew MacLaren in full cry.

In March 1935 MacLaren wrote a pamphlet on the distressed areas in Scotland, South Wales, West Cumberland and Tyneside. The effects of the economic depression were felt there most keenly and they must also be included in the 'doctors' mandate' given to the government. The Commissioners of the Distressed Areas were to be given an annual sum of £2 million. The recommendations of the Commissioners of the four areas included transfer of unemployed, training of youths, public works, land settlement, subsidies, national public assistance, and other schemes which in MacLaren's opinion would 'not so much as touch the fringe of the problem.' He identified the underlying problem as an unjust distribution of wealth. Regional policy was, he felt, really something to fool, first the politicians, and then the electorate. Land value was a natural reflection of the demand for its use. It was unjust for those living where it was low, and where the benefit of the community was lowest, that it should be assessed on the same basis as those living where communal advantages were greater. If taxation were imposed on land value, MacLaren contended, the poverty in both locations would be remedied. Through enormous expenditure the odd road was built. But it was rarely used. The English Commissioner, Sir Michael Stewart admitted the idea had 'generally speaking ... failed.'[1] It is impossible to benefit

---

[1] Taylor, A.J.P., *English History 1914–45*, p. 437.

one region without seeing the landlord collect the windfall. In Scotland the farthest parts, like the Western Isles and the Highlands, suffered from mass emigration.

This was an era of official reports, of campaigns to 'produce more' and of 'emigration to the colonies.' Thomas, as Minister of Employment, announced that wooden railway sleepers would be replaced by steel ones, in order to revive the steel industry.

In February 1933 Neville Chamberlain told the Commons that since 1924 until September 1931 about £100,000 per annum had been spent on public schemes to relieve unemployment and the number of unemployed had still risen from 1.2 million to 2.8 million. The steel, iron, air, shipbuilding industries were reorganised, amalgamated and protected.

The Liberal ministers and Snowden threatened to resign. But a compromise was reached by which they remained in the Cabinet with the freedom of opposition on the trade issue. In February 1931 Neville Chamberlain introduced the Import Duties Bill and paid a pious tribute to his father, Jo, who had been the founder of Tariff Reform in 1903. The Act imposed a general tariff of 10 per cent and set up the Import Duties Advisory Committee. Protectionists now held a substantial majority in the Cabinet and they lost no time in rushing through an Abnormal Importations Bill, in November 1931, to allow a tariff to be imposed up to 100 per cent against 'abnormal' quantities of imported goods. Orders were made against imports of iron and steel, radio parts, electric lights, cameras, bottles, woollen and cotton goods, typewriters, cutlery and pottery.

Agriculture was assisted by the Wheat Act 1932, the Sugar Industry (Reorganisation) Act 1935 and the formation of a number of Marketing Boards. MacLaren perceived that State assistance of agriculture was destined to swell the receipts of landowners. Sure enough, the Import Duties Advisory Committee recommended that the general tariff should be raised to 20 per cent. Over three years they heard 300 requests of which they prescribed protection in 100 cases.

A docile and fearful electorate allowed this miserable measure to go without fight or even public debate. Comparing the lofty inspiration of Cobden and eloquence of young Churchill with the weak argument of Chamberlain was tragic to MacLaren. It was as if a parliament of long history, spirited oratory and noble tradition had been pillaged by a foe with no respect for it.

The Liberals and Snowden had earlier protested at protectionist measures and the doctrine of collective cabinet responsibility on the issue gave way to majority decisions and a specious compromise which allowed ministers to speak on their own behalf.

In August 1932 the National Government agreed at Ottawa to sweeping protectionism and to Imperial preferences. The measures were symbolic; an ending of free trade but not, as Chamberlain had hoped, the introduction of Empire Free Trade.

The illusory concept of Empire Free Trade was frustrated by Baldwin's refusal to impose 'stomach taxes' against food imported from outside the Empire and by his demand for British preference within the Empire by the raising of tariffs against non-British trade.

In September 1932, Snowden, Sir Herbert Samuel, Sir Archibald Sinclair and eight junior ministers resigned from the National Government because they considered it had become a Tory protectionist racket. Yet the Liberal Party went into hibernation over the issue. The concept of the 'National Interest' seduced the House from honesty and plain speaking.

MacDonald was surrounded, as he feared, by Conservative Protectionists. He sought to end his international economic problems at the World Economic Conference held in June 1933 in London. But the Conference was a failure. In 1933 the economy revived and unemployment, which had peaked at 3.4 million, fell to nearly two and a half million. By 1937 it had fallen to 1.8 million.

The National Government instituted a new regime of post-free trade policies. A managed currency, cheap money and tariffs. In July 1932 the Exchange Equalisation Fund was created to allow the State to fix the exchange value of sterling. However, devaluation of the pound sparked an American and French devaluation and little was achieved by it other than a disruption of trade. France lead other smaller nations off the Gold Standard. Bank interest rates were set at 2 per cent in June 1932, where they remained until 1951. This did not, however, stimulate investment; interest rates were only a very minor factor when there was no profit incentive. Public spending was curtailed by the financial orthodoxy of a balanced budget. Tariffs were employed to divert trade to the Empire. Britain demanded preference with her colonies. This was a selfish and futile demand for though it might have sheltered industry in Britain for a few years it made her uncompetitive in the world. Neither use of tariffs nor the low interest rates achieved any measurable gain.

Keynes launched his concept of planning in his *Treatise of Money*, published in 1930, and in 1936 in his *General Theory of Employment*. Keynes gave government a new theory together with the tools to impress it on society. MacLaren regarded him as a caricature of a thinker; full of anxieties, partial remedies, sentimentality and enthused by belief in himself. He saw him as a pathetic man who held the notion that man could ignore Nature and yet attempt to outdo her.

MacLaren was particularly critical of the National Government. 'There is nothing more pathetic than this 'National Government,' he once said, 'the Socialist and Labour representatives in it make my heart weep. Greater hypocrisy could never have existed. It is only England that could tolerate such hypocrisy as a National Government, which is supposed to represent different political facets of the State. Just look at them. It is a Tory administration, and those who are not official Tories are lackeys and sycophants who are running after the office they enjoy. There is one of them sitting there now. We are told that these are the people who are devoted to doing something for the State and offering their lives to the State. All I know is that there are men sitting on the Front Bench drawing a considerable sum at the end of the year and who would not draw one third of it if they were out of public life. If they were attending their own funerals tomorrow they would not be missed.'[1]

The Tory ministers tried to tack the clauses of repeal of the land valuation provisions onto the Budgets of 1932 and 1933. But Baldwin, who was not at all sympathetic to the valuation proposals, stopped these manoeuvres, as a matter of honesty, for which he was noted. However, the tenacity of the Tories

---
[1] Hansard, col. 713 12:4:37.

prevailed and the valuation was scrapped in 1934. Snowden told the Press: 'I suppose this has been done at the instigation of the Prime Minister, who wants to give further proof of the thoroughness of his conversion to Toryism.'[1]

The United Committee for the Taxation of Land Value wrote to MacDonald to protest. He replied with what a Liberal Member called a 'nauseating hypocrisy'.[2] First, he said that he anticipated the repeal would provoke a useful debate of the issue. Secondly, that the clauses had never been in operation. Although, in fact, the valuation was going ahead and Snowden predicted that by 1934 it would be completed. Finally, he suggested that the exemptions allowed by Snowden were in any event too wide to achieve the purposes of the Bill.[3] Snowden described the contents of this letter as an 'incoherent jumble of nonsense'.[4]

Viscount Snowden, as he had become, described in the Lords the repeal of the taxation of land valuation principles as 'an act of deliberate Party deception . . . of deliberate sharp practice . . . the latest of many which show the true character of this government and exposed its hypocrisy to be called a National Government.'[5]

Snowden, reflecting on the villainy of the MacDonald era, said: 'All the signs of the times point to the fact that the tragic experiences of war have taught the statesmen of Europe no lesson except to prepare on a more colossal scale and with feverish activity for the repetition of that terrible calamity'.[6] He attacked MacDonald from the cross benches of the House of Lords: 'Whatever profession he [MacDonald] ever made, whatever pledges he gave, there is no humiliation to which he will not submit if they only allow him to be called Prime Minister.' Lord Sankey implored Snowden to moderate his bitter words but Snowden remained impassive and silent.

He had always been an unusual figure in Parliament. Partially crippled since his youth by spinal tuberculosis he resembled, it

---

[1] Snowden, P., *Autobiography*, vol. 2, p. 919.
[2] Hansard (Lords) vol. 93, col. 291.
[3] Ibid., col. 290.
[4] Ibid., col. 290.
[5] Ibid., col. 291.
[6] Snowden, P., *Autobiography*, vol. 2, p. 1040.

was often remarked, Robespierre. But he had a precise articulation and could, even in his retirement, dictate a newspaper article of 2000 words over the telephone without repeating himself. In his last public speech in November 1934, he had said: 'There is no social or economic question which is not at bottom a land question ... It is from the land all our essential needs are supplied, and if that essential source is monopolised, if there are a few individuals who can control that supply, then they hold the destiny in their hands.'

In 1935 he wrote to the Henry George Conference in the United States: 'The root cause of the world's economic distress is surely obvious to every man who has eyes to see and a brain to understand. So long as land is a monopoly and men are denied free access to it to apply their labour to its uses, poverty and unemployment will exist.' MacLaren observed how politicians who were weak when in power become veritable bulldogs when retired.

Unemployment assistance was further complicated by the hated means test. Chamberlain attempted to remove it from politics altogether in the Unemployment Act 1934, by transferring its administration to the Unemployment Assistance Board.

In June 1935 MacDonald resigned in favour of Baldwin. In November MacLaren was returned in the General Election to represent Burslem again with a 3000 majority. The Labour Party returned 154 and the Conservatives 387. The issues of the campaign were domestic; the people did not care much for the question of rearmament – a programme costing only £100 million per annum for the next four years – or for the situation in Abyssinia.

MacLaren declared himself an opponent of poverty, vested interests and militarism.

> You cannot be an effective opponent of war if you do not connect the causes of war with the economic causes which give rise to the war mind ... It is no good talking piously about the League of Nations and then say you are going to stop nations trading ... Mussolini is trying to get more territory in Abyssinia by murder and plunder and do not let

us be too unctuous. Let us remember that we in this country are not altogether free of the charge that, in the past, the British Empire was built by the same procedure . . . I charge the National Government – and I charge any champion of the National Government to deny it – with bringing us to the state we are in. Comparing the state of the world with that of 1931, there were more armies marching than in the history of mankind. Protection, launched by the only country that stood for the free exchange of goods and services between men, was the cause of it. The Conference of Ottawa was for the purpose of making the Empire a closed shop, blocking out the trade of foreign countries. Could anything have been more vicious and likely to invite the hatred of other countries – What was the result of that? The road to Adous, Abyssinia [the point of Mussolini's invasion] is through Ottawa.[1]

The Labour Party had an emotional appeal for the League of Nations and they backed its every deliberation while hoping, piously and naively, that economic sanctions would block Mussolini.

When Mosley had failed to make any impression with his New Party he hurried, in January 1932, to Mussolini in Rome in search of inspiration. On his return he founded the British Union of Fascists, publishing his programme, *The Greater Britain*. It outlined a puerile scheme of state control. The element of anti-Semitism became more evident after the death of his first wife, Cynthia. His fascist rabble enjoyed a membership of 20,000 at its highest point. If anyone personified the 'devil's decade', as the 1930s were often called, it was Mosley. MacLaren was wary from the start when they began wearing the uniform of blackshirts, which they adapted after the example of Mussolini. He sensed what effect uniforms would have among the poor and unemployed at a time when the world seemed to drift from one uncertainty to another. The Fascists were a pathetic rabble. They were given to shows of brute strength at meetings and during processions, which were conducted mainly through the Jewish

---

[1] *Evening Sentinel*, 4:11:35.

parts of the East End of London. Their proceedings constituted a gross violation of liberty and public pressure forced the government to curtail the freedom to hold processions.

MacLaren spoke in the debate on the Public Order Bill of 1936, which had been introduced to outlaw the blackshirts. He suggested that the House should require public movements to be obliged to disclose their sources of finance, and strengthen democracy by removing poverty which unsettled society. Lord Rothermere and many respectable Conservatives applauded Mosley. MacLaren felt the Bill had achieved great publicity and Mosley would be happiest about that. He felt the House was over-reacting. The Bill banned the blackshirt uniform and curtailed the freedom to hold processions. MacLaren saw the uniform as the token of poverty; it could be banned but the poverty would remain.

Similar plaudits were bestowed on Hitler. He was, it was said, the saviour of Germany. Again MacLaren was not deceived. He saw him a figure raised from the murky pond of poverty. He was more interested in the rottenness of the economic conditions that nurtured him than in the man himself.

In a debate on the Civil List 1936, MacLaren ventured a suggestion regarding royal presentation. 'I never look on a Royal procession coming to this House for the opening of Parliament but I deeply regret the military glamour of the thing. It would be well if Royalty in this country would identify more with the scientific, industrial and artistic activities of the State, instead of having cordons of soldiers, the rattling of sabres, gun carriages. It would be more in keeping with the nation of Shakespeare if they were surrounded by members of the artistic and educational and craft guilds of the State, instead of a retinue of military, which is quite foreign to the character of the people of this country.'[1]

Snowden, one of the few champions of land value taxation and free trade, died in June 1937; MacDonald five months later. Thomas, MacDonald's bagman, had been expelled from the House of Commons for being found guilty of leaking a Budget secret before the Budget of 1936.

Maxton, a radical Labour Member, also admitted to MacLaren

---

[1] Hansard, col. 1629, 5:5:36.

on his death bed that all he had been saying about land was true, although it had not seemed to him so at the time. Like Snowden, absence from the tumble of politics had concentrated his mind on fundamental ideas. But MacLaren regretted that their reflection was delayed too long to be put to the practical problems with which they were confronted.

In 1937 Baldwin retired and Neville Chamberlain became Prime Minister. He inherited Baldwin's ministers. 'He was the least glamorous of prime ministers: efficient, conscientious and unimaginative.'[1]

MacLaren won the chance to introduce a Bill to the House in 1937 and by an unpredictable rush of blood to the brain he chose to introduce the Land Values (Rating) Bill. Local authorities were to be given the option to adopt land value rating. At the next quinquennial valuation after adoption of the Act there were to be three changes. First, the rating valuation lists were expanded by one more column to show the annual site value of every hereditament in the rating list. Secondly, agricultural land was restored to the list but became liable to annual site value rating only and not to existing rates. Thirdly, rating authorities were empowered to transfer the rating burden progressively from the existing system to the annual site value. Annual site value was defined as the price of a perpetual annuity which the fee simple might produce on a sale, on the assumption that all buildings, improvements and works, except roads and natural growth, were growing on the land. In other words, the annual site value of land ignored every vestige of human improvement wrought on that site and concentrated on the simple value of land which a community created.

The ingenious resort to perpetual annuities really was no more than a device to direct a valuer to concentrate when valuing a heraditament, or property, on the selling price of bare site value; to direct him to ignore buildings and improvements on the particular property which he is valuing. Thus if he were valuing a fine agricultural estate he would ignore the existence of the buildings, the improvements, the crops, the felling value of trees, game rights and the like and imagine in his mind all that

---

[1] Taylor, A.J.P., *English History 1914–45*, p. 497.

was on the site was natural growth and all around the site was a community in its existing state. In other words, to value only what is due to communal presence.

In promoting his Bill, MacLaren traced the history of poverty. It had emerged from the ruinous spoliation and enclosures of the Tudors. It had given rise to the Elizabethan Poor Law of 1601 and was intensified by the enclosures of the eighteenth century, which also gave rise to the workhouse. That remained essentially unaltered until the emergence in the present century of what MacLaren was accustomed to call the 'make-up' state.

Wedgwood, another campaigner for the taxation of land values, spoke in support of the Bill. He contrasted the growth of Sydney, which derived all its taxation from land values, with Melbourne, which rated buildings as in the United Kingdom. In 1900 the two cities were of comparable size but since the adoption of land values taxation, Sydney had forged ahead.

The opposition case was put by Henry Raikes. He referred to what the Cadbury family had done to Bournville and could cite, he said, many other examples. He contrasted the cases of the man who developed his land to the full and made himself liable to higher tax and the owner who held his land underdeveloped and made himself liable to very little tax. In fact both would pay the same and the latter would be forced to develop in quick time. Mr. Donner seconded the opposition. He contested that God never gave the land to the People and called MacLaren's recitation of history 'childish'. Land ownership had gone hand-in-hand with human progress. Land may have been held communally at some early stage of society under a system of primitive communism. But such a system hardly suited modern conditions. The tax would be wasteful of capital and individual effort.

There was no sense of understanding in the House and the Bill failed to obtain a second reading. A year later, the House of Commons rejected Herbert Morrison's Site Value Rating Bill – London Rating (Site Values) (1938–9) – which had been drafted by the London County Council. It defined annual site value as the rental value of the land on a perpetually renewable lease with vacant possession without regard being had to any buildings, improvements or the like on the site on a perpetual lease.

Though this calculation of site value seemed more direct, the valuation of rental value might prove more difficult than the deduction of rental value from capital value.

An attempt was later made to present the measure as a private Bill but the Speaker ruled it was a public one. It was re-introduced under the 10 minute rule and rejected on second reading by a majority of 194. Since then the House of Commons has not been troubled by similar bills.

The taxation of land values had once captured the country's imagination and precipitated a great constitutional crisis in 1909–11; it had inspired a Labour Government to act decisively in 1931; but it was all but buried during the 1930s.

In 1785, Condorcet wrote that Turgot believed unless a person understood the principle of land value taxation, he would not understand much about government. Yet its principal argument stands today. It still underlies every economic question in society.

MacLaren saw the falsity in the premises of the Budget. It was pretended to effect changes in the distribution of wealth. But it did not take from the rich and give to the poor. 'All taxation at present,' he declared, 'is extracted from the common pool of wealth produced by those who work in the production of wealth, and when we are told that the working classes, owing to their small incomes, are therefore paying very little in taxation, I say that is a travesty of the facts.'[1] Taxes were levied on specific fiscal targets, but when passed into the price system, they were paid in the main by the mass of the population.

MacLaren saw little in the passing party political scene to cheer him; it revealed the fulfilment of much that he had foreseen himself. He retained the same wit and passion which had such marked qualities in his political life; quick to expose the pretensions and humbug of public figures and to mock human foibles.

---

[1] Hansard, col. 834, 3:5:38.

13

Second World War

In 1939 the situation in Europe grew darker and darker. Knowing the course of events, with hindsight, dulls the horror as it would have unfolded month after month.

MacLaren was deeply affected. He had always dreaded what, to him, was possible while so many were unemployed and poverty stricken. He went along hopefully with the policy of appeasement; any policy which avoided war. War in his mind did not occur because a villain like Hitler suddenly came out of a blue sky. Hitler arose in a society shadowed by poverty; a fertile breeding ground for anti-Semitism and jingoism. MacLaren could see the signs of another war but he hoped for a miracle to avert one.

'Sooner or later, [Chamberlain] believed, Hitler and Mussolini would be begging for forgiveness, if Anthony Eden [the Foreign Secretary] continued to wag his finger at them.'[1] In fact Eden kept up his stance of 'impotent disapproval',[2] but dictators do not respond to diplomatic finger wagging.

In February 1939 MacLaren pleaded for the statesmen of Europe to have the courage to settle the matter before Europe found itself engulfed again in the mindless desolation of war. In March Hitler entered Austria with brutal disregard for liberty and peace. In September the Germans in Czechoslovakia revolted. On 29 September Chamberlain went to Munich with some hope that he could prevent an invasion of Czechoslovakia by redressing German grievances by proposing the expansion of

---
[1] Taylor, A.J.P., *English History 1914–45*, p. 516.
[2] Ibid., p. 518.

the German Sudetenland. He returned with a piece of paper. The paper expressed a desire of Germany and Britain not to go to war against each other. The Commons liked it. The press, the people, the Dominions liked it too.

MacLaren praised Neville Chamberlain for his efforts to conclude peace at Munich in September 1938. 'God bless the Prime Minister,' he declared from the bottom of his heart, 'for what he did in Munich. We are here today discussing this passively because he had the singular courage to do what he did.'[1] This heartfelt tribute offended the petty socialist party officials who sought to dismiss MacLaren from the party. MacLaren made light of their actions by forming the BBC – the 'bell, book and candle' for members who had been threatened with expulsion by their parties. Sir Stafford Cripps, Maxton and the ILP were enrolled and membership was also offered to Eden, Duff Cooper and Churchill, who were each known to have had difficulties with their party.

In fact, MacLaren had marked the Prime Minister's announcement of his flying visit to Munich, by drawing his face on a cigarette packet, as he was addressing the House. He later transcribed it to a more appropriate medium. Lansbury and others offered to subscribe for it in order to keep it in the House. But a Government whip discovered a rule that no picture of a living member could be exhibited. Sir William Brass eventually paid 20 guineas for it which MacLaren donated to the Hayward Hospital in Burslem.

Later the *Sunday Times* commissioned MacLaren to draw a more formal picture of the Prime Minister. He studied Chamberlain's features closely and, in doing so, recognised a similar sound in his throat that he had heard from Bonar Law. It was a symptom of cancer of the throat. He had nearly finished the drawing when the debate on Norway was held in May 1940. The Prime Minister spoke, and the front bench, which only weeks before, had been overflowing with members hoping for a job, was empty. During the debate a Tory shouted 'Go! For God's sake go!' at the Prime Minister. At the end of the debate MacLaren crossed the floor in order to reach the Tory front

---

[1] Hansard, col. 107, 20:2:39.

bench. Chamberlain looked up like a wounded animal. MacLaren offered his arm and advised him to leave. They walked arm in arm down from an astonished Chamber to the Yard where his wife, who had been listening in the visitors' gallery, and who was aware of his health, stood, too shattered to speak, with tears streaming down her cheeks. She was a very beautiful woman and the tears, MacLaren thought, made her appear more striking. As Chamberlain stood on the running board of his car he turned to thank MacLaren. 'Maclaren,' he said, 'I have learned a lot about human nature these last six weeks.' MacLaren felt that remark hit him like a hammer.

MacLaren completed the drawing and was requested to send it round to Downing Street. The Prime Minister wrote at the foot of the original that it was the best drawing of him that he knew.

MacLaren became haunted by Chamberlain's looks, which stared at him in his studio. He was only too happy to give it to the National Portrait Gallery when they requested it. Long after the war, in his late eighties, he once visited the Gallery to enquire whether photocopies of it could be obtained. A rather stout lady said there were a few available. She said he could take three for 11 shillings each. He promptly demanded a free one. The lady was taken aback by his request. 'You see,' said MacLaren mischievously, 'I drew it. I do not think it is right for you to live off the labour of others.' The woman's jaw dropped in astonishment and then she smiled with delight. 'Please,' cautioned MacLaren, 'don't propose to me in public.'

In March 1939 Czechoslovakia was invaded. The word of Hitler could not be trusted. Slowly the British nation was stirred to war. It was finally triggered when Hitler invaded Poland on 25 August, forcing the government to declare war on 3 September.

In May 1940 Churchill replaced Chamberlain as Prime Minister. At last the National Government, which had been cobbled together to meet the financial crisis of 1931, passed out of existence. A sustained diminuendo had finally come to its end. In 1941 MacLaren recalled the fateful moment when Europe went to war again. He was speaking against a compulsory National Service Bill.

Tonight we are seeing the fruits of the conduct that has been carried on upon that [Conservative] side of the House for the last 20 years or so. Little did you think of this when you rushed headlong into tariffs in 1931 and when I alone – for which I take no credit – pleaded with the Tories opposite. 'Do not do this thing, because, if you rush into tariffs, you paralyse international trade on earth and, as sure as day follows night, there will be a war the like of which mankind has never known.' You ran into the Aye lobby to the sound of little tinkling bells, because you thought you were beginning a new order with your tariffs against the foreigner; little did you think you were beginning a new era of international hatred. Little did you think, after your Ottawa Conference, when you prided yourselves, that you were going to make the British Empire a closed shop against the earth.[1]

In the debate for the conscription of women MacLaren said he was saddened by such a pass. Much use had been made of the example of Russian women rushing to the defence of their country.

Why did the Russians, to a man, enlist to defend Russia? Because it is their country, but because in this country a landless people, you have to conscript their bodies to defend it. If this land had belonged to the people of Great Britain, this Bill would not become necessary . . . At least we can make a resolution that, if we survive, we do not intend to witness in the past, namely, those who have gone out to defend the centre of this mighty Empire gradually found their way to the edge of the pavements, displaying their medals playing their instruments and begging for charity.[2]

MacLaren was concerned that women whose male folk were away at war had to go to work in factories and desert their homes.

---

[1] Ibid., col. 1788–9; 11:12:41.
[2] Ibid., col. 1790 11:12:41.

During the War, MacLaren worked under his former school friend, Sir Andrew Duncan. He was responsible for two Ordnance factories in Swynerton and at Radway Green, in Staffordshire, to where the Woolwich Arsenal had been evacuated. At first the men were housed in lodgings. MacLaren foresaw that when the bombing started the older and more skilled men would want to return to their families. So in the space of a few days he worked with his architect in Stoke-on-Trent, George Greaves, to submit a plan to house about 300 families. The plan was accepted by Duncan and executed immediately.

He was also responsible for representing the Minister in such operations as bomb damage repair. The State had armed itself with powers reminiscent of the *ancien régime* in pre-revolutionary France. It simply commandeered building workers in a totally arbitrary fashion. Small builders were devastated by this sudden plunder of their resources. MacLaren grouped them into a Federation which made a rotational offering of resources to the State.

MacLaren also proved to be an effective strike-breaker. Some builders from London were sent to work alongside workers from the Potteries in Coventry. The London workers were accustomed to formal tea breaks, whereas the local men were happy to have on-site breaks in order to save the time needed to leave the site. The leader of the London workers, a Communist, spluttered his indignation at MacLaren and vehemently threatened a strike. MacLaren listened to him and when the man had finished he read him a report in that day's *Times* of a battle in the Greek mountains. It was a moving eye-witness account of terrible cold and injuries. Then he asked the men if any of their friends or relations were fighting in Greece. They immediately returned to work.

On another occasion MacLaren was lectured by a Trade Union official who was bent on calling a strike. Asked which union he belonged to the leader said he was from the Engineer's Society. MacLaren demanded to see his card but the man had not got it even though he was required by the union rules to carry it at all times. MacLaren produced his own and ruled that the dispute was at an end.

MacLaren rarely spoke in the House during the war. The fight was a serious business once it commenced and he left its direction to Members with more knowledge of military operations. As the end of the struggle began to loom, however, the House became preoccupied with the task of reconstruction. MacLaren had seen the shambles which had followed the First War and he was determined to do all he could to avert a repeat.

> Are you now going to ask these men [he demanded], that come back from the bloody battlefields, broken, shattered, or at least with an experience they would have been better without; are we going to ask the women to come from factories after being divorced from the quiet domestic atmosphere of their homes; are we going to ask the common people of England to come back from this enterprise, having accomplished the defeat of these people who would have taken this land, to crawl through it as mere tenants, as tributary to the owners to the soil? . . . [I suggest] that every one of us in this House must have a new spiritual outlook. It is not enough to talk of working men and of employers, as if God intended men to be nothing more nor less than creatures engaged in some eternal factory process. Behind the eye of every human you gaze at there is a human soul. It is to save the soul of man that we fight for economic justice to liberate men from mere necessity of physical requirements, so that his soul can rise to higher planes . . . Let us not be easily trapped into these schemes [of reconstruction] . . . because we may be ensnared into economic slavery in the guise of being well fed and well housed.[1]

MacLaren believed freedom was the essential foundation of man's existence.

In June 1942 MacLaren drew attention to a letter in the *Times* from Sir William Beveridge. 'I feel as if something ought to be done about this gentleman. He is one of the most dangerous bureaucrats walking about in our time.'[2]

---

[1] Ibid., 2:12:42.
[2] Ibid., col. 1878; 23:6:42.

MacLaren had often dismissed the idea of the welfare state, whose creation owed more to Beveridge than anyone, as a massive delusion. It attempted to mitigate social disease of poverty while at the same time leaving its cause undisturbed.

It mattered not to MacLaren that the whole nation wanted to believe in the welfare state. It was out of accord with Nature because it was financed by the taxpayer. As MacLaren observed, taxes, other than the one he favoured, were passed on into the price of goods and services. Thus the burden would fall most heavily on the poor for whose very benefit the welfare was intended. The price would be felt in unemployment and more extreme poverty. Rather than gape wondrously at a hospital, comforting oneself that it provided a free service, the taxpayer had better remind himself that he was paying for it even when he was well and had no need of it.

I wish to protest [he had told the House in 1931] that I have never heard anything more fatuous than the idea that a bureaucracy can come and collect money from individuals' pockets and spend it far better than can the individuals themselves. It arises from the fallacious idea that it is the function of the State to bring about something like equality in the distribution of wealth. Instead of removing the injustices which give rise to the maldistribution of wealth.[1]

Beveridge had suggested that 'the greatest cause of poverty in this country is young children (sic).' Nothing provoked MacLaren more than this sort of fatuous claim.

Does anyone in the House believe that? Yet this man is the inspirer of economic wisdom of the Government – I never meet a university professor but I want to run round looking for a loaded revolver. This gentleman has taken the place of my dear old friend Sydney Webb. He works with the greatest industry but always on the wrong premises. He reminds me of what Buckle said about the Scottish clergy of the sixteenth century, that there were no men more erudite,

---
[1] Ibid., col. 749 2:10:31.

but, having started on the wrong premises, the greater their erudition, the greater their ignorance.[1]

In November 1942 the Beveridge Report on social reconstruction was published. Beveridge aimed to destroy the 'five giants' of Want, Disease, Ignorance, Squalor and Idleness. It is a sad commentary on what MacLaren termed 'the bappy state' of public opinion during wartime that this plausive, vain academic was believed. Indeed as he wrote: 'The public boom in this Report is overwhelming. I became at a blow, one of the best known characters in the country.'[2] His ideas took Keynes like a storm at night. It 'leaves me', he enthused, 'in a wild state of excitement. I think it is a vast, constructive reform of real importance and am relieved that it is so financially possible.'[3]

But Beveridge was so inspired by his mighty dream that he hardly bothered about its costs which he estimated, starting at £86 million per annum, would only 'slightly rise' by 1965! In fact, it doubled within two years of its full implementation. The report was based on a survey done in seven towns between the wars. This survey purported to show that 75 per cent of poverty was due to loss of income and 25 per cent to inability to live within one's means. Economic thinking had come to depend on statistics rather than reasoned argument.

The Beveridge Report started grandly by proclaiming that: 'A revolutionary moment in the world's history is a time for revolutions, not patching up.'[4] It recommended child allowances of five shillings a week and a comprehensive health service.

A flavour of Beveridge's thinking can be gleaned from his tract *Full Employment in a Free Society*. 'Bargaining for wages must be responsible, looking not to snatching short term sectional advantages, but to the permanent good of the whole community[5] . . . It is better to employ people on digging holes and filling them up, than not to employ them at all; those who are taken into useless employment will, by what they earn and

---
[1] Ibid.
[2] Beveridge, Sir W., *Power and Influence*, p. 319.
[3] Ibid., p. 309.
[4] Cmnd 6404, p. 6.
[5] Ibid., 23.

spend, give employment to others.[1] ... Acceptance of this new responsibility [of the State making consumer demand] marks the line we must cross, in order to pass from the old Britain of unemployment to the new Britain of opportunity and service for all.'[2]

MacLaren attended a meeting addressed by Beveridge at Friends' House. MacLaren asked him what was the cause of unemployment. The learned bureaucrat, who had mesmerised Churchill in 1910 with his idea of labour exchanges, paused to collect his wisdom. At length, he suggested there were many, but most lay outside the direct control of government. They required an army of bureaucrats, or tea drinkers, as MacLaren referred to them.

Let us not be trapped into these schemes that are put in front of us because we may be ensnared into economic slavery in the guise of being well fed and well housed. The men who are now in the vortex of conflict beyond this House are fighting for liberty; let it not be said that the politicians were unworthy of the great sacrifices of those noble fellows and were selling their liberty and substituting for that liberty State control.[3]

Keynes presented himself as a liberal. He was a thoroughgoing dirigiste, managing a state, as if it was a corporation. He felt that *laissez-faire* was out of fashion and 'that the ideal size for a unit of control ... lies somewhere between the individual and the modern state ... The transition from economic anarchy to a regime which is deliberately aimed at controlling and directing economic forces in the interests of justice and social stability ... I believe that the right solution [to economic problems] will involve intellectual and scientific elements which must be above the heads of the vast mass of more or less literate voters.'

Through Lord Home, MacLaren met his brother William Douglas-Home. William shared his brother's sense of humour.

---
[1] Ibid., 47.
[2] Ibid., 29.
[3] Hansard, col. 1222, 2:12:42.

'Maybe Alec thought I was half daft and should meet his brother' MacLaren surmised. He understood William to be a conscientious objector at the outbreak of the Second World War. So he was surprised in 1942 to open the door of his studio to find William wearing the uniform of an officer in the Royal Artillery Company. William tried to counter MacLaren's surprise by saying that he had determined not to wage war against civilians. MacLaren was not convinced of this determination. Once enlisted, thought MacLaren, an individual lost personal authority. However, William did later disobey an order to move tanks into occupied Le Havre. He was court martialled and spent a year in Wormwood Scrubs. While there, he wrote a play called *New Barabbas* and MacLaren went to its premier at Bilton's Theatre, in London.

In 1943 MacLaren attended a function in the Midlands with Aneurin Bevin to introduce the National Health Service. On the train back to London, Bevin asked MacLaren to explain the land question. As they neared London, Bevin grasped the whole argument. Yet he remarked that the pension funds of the Trade Unions had invested so heavily in land that they would never listen to the taxation of land value. MacLaren thought being blinded by these interests was like a bird choosing to remain in a cage merely to please its gaoler. Politicians do not like loosening their hold on power as a result of threatening vested interests, yet MacLaren believed that rather than be able to use power for the benefit of society, politicians become mere playthings of powerful interests. They might hold power but they were not powerful.

He quoted Gracchi addressing the returning legionaries in ancient Rome. 'You have gone abroad,' he said, 'you have vanquished. You have come now to the Imperial city with the trimmings of victory swinging on your banners – to return to cellars which even your horses would refuse to inhabit.'[1]

MacLaren often criticised the BBC for broadcasting sentimental trivia, crooners and jazz. He listened to concerts of music by Mozart, Hadyn and other classical composers whenever they were broadcast but felt that a country which had reared

---
[1] Ibid., col. 875, 7:12:44.

Shakespeare and a host of poets and musicians deserved to be better served than the BBC's wireless output often suggested.

He was anxious to expose the official humbug of state bureaucracy. He recounted the recruitment of one man in the Ministry of Information. The ministry servants demanded to know what the man could do. The answer was that he knew a lot about music having been an organist all his life. The man was asked to make a submission as to what he would do for war propaganda. He sat down for half a day and finally produced a sheet of note paper on which he had written: 'When you are having propaganda go all out for it. At each meeting have 'Hope and Glory!' When the principal speaker goes on, have the National Anthem, after he sits down, the 'Hallelujah Chorus' and 'Auld Lang Syne' at the finish.'[1] In bringing this state of affairs to the attention of the House, MacLaren said: 'Publicity requires a handsome imagination, it requires an appreciation of the psychology of the people to whom you are making the appeal and you must amalgamate with the appeal a sense of art, which I am sorry is almost dead in this country ... These atrophied mummies ... have no sense of these aesthetic qualities.'[2]

He was amused by the ease with which architects crept into Whitehall. Indeed the creation of the Ministry of Town and Country Planning was greeted as a special boon. 'When the facts [regarding it's creation] became more definitely known the "Aribas" foregathered. Yes, there is to be a Town and Country Planning Ministry! Professor Abercrombie immediately drew his sword from its scabbard and shouted "Charge!" What happened? The "Aribas" made straight for St. James Square.'[3]

MacLaren felt increasingly unhappy in the Labour Party. He had joined the ILP in 1914 and seen it adopt sensible ideas like free trade and land value taxation. But the party had been destroyed, largely by MacDonald and his foil Thomas. MacLaren once saw the latter playing cards with the railway bosses and distrusted him from the start considering him a matineé artist.

---

[1] Ibid., col. 411, 12:10:39.
[2] Ibid., col. 412.
[3] Ibid., col. 299–300, 15:3:44.

MacLaren's disappointment in the Labour leadership was shared by Lansbury. Lansbury was a big-hearted soul, but more, he embraced manly and radical policies. He was broken by the decline of the party.

In March 1943, Thomas Williams, the parliamentary secretary of the Minister of Agriculture, sponsored a bill to compensate landowners after the war. There was, however, to be no compensation for parents of children lost in the war. This was the last straw for MacLaren. He wrote to the parliamentary party chairman, Arthur Greenwood. He was no admirer of Greenwood. In the name of party unity Labour members were expected to overlook Greenwood's drink problem; he was, after all, Minister of Health. MacLaren wrote:

9 March 1943
Dear Mr. Greenwood,
For a number of years in the House of Commons it has been noticeable that in parliamentary action the Labour Party has attempted to mitigate the results of poverty by compromises and political expedients which did not fundamentally challenge the root causes of poverty and economic insecurity. True, as a Party it has not had the numerical strength to enforce its will upon the legislation of the Country, but, be that as it may, the general line of attack upon basic social wrongs has lacked a clear conception of what these basic causes of poverty are, and what constitutional action should be taken to remove them.

The disinterested enthusiasm and faith of the working classes in the Country can only be sustained if, through constitutional and parliamentary action, the root causes of their economic insecurity are vigorously opposed and definite solutions embodied in legislative proposals are advanced by their representatives in Parliament.

There is a danger that by the promotion of policies savour more of the State reliefs than of direct challenges to these basic social wrongs, the liberty of the individual will be compromised by the growth of state officialdom.

The test of the future, as I see it, is how best to expand the rights of the community as a community and at the same time preserve the rights and liberties of the individual. To foster one at the expense of the other is to lead to disappointment and the uprising of revolutionary movements.

It has been my distressing experience in the House of Commons to hear some of my own colleagues deriding the principles of free trade, and the destruction of land speculation through the instrumentality of taxation. For many years there has been within the Party a group whose views on the land question were distinctly reactionary, and I have had some experience of opposition from this group when I have tried to influence party opinion on the necessity for a radical change in the whole conception of land ownership.

Believing that all men have equal rights to life, which implies the equal rights of all human beings to the enjoyment of those gifts freely provided by nature and necessary to man's existence – land, light, water and air – I hold that it is the first and primary duty of the workers' representatives in Parliament to destroy utterly the private ownership in any of these elements. To allow the basis of wealth production – natural resources – to remain in absolute private ownership means a continual army of unemployed whose presence in the labour market compete with and force down the wages of those in employment; gives rise to speculation around towns, and condemns millions of other people to live in the slums, checking all health development and necessitating vast health expenditure.

Holding such opinions and observing how little they seem to be present in the minds of others, I become a little dismayed when I see an increased tendency towards State doles and charity schemes while these basic wrongs exist unchallenged.

The war has short-circuited time. Millions returning from the battlefields and the factories will expect a better recompense for the sacrifices they have made in the defence of their Country than those embodied in the proposals that have so far been discussed in Parliament. It is my devout hope that the unique opportunity now to hand in the drive towards Social Justice will not find the working-class movement lacking in vision, understanding and determination.

The principles I advocate are embodied in past declarations of policy of the Labour Party. If these principles are no longer vital to the Party then I have no alternative but to withdraw from the Party in the House, not in any sense of bitterness, but rather in the hope that a better day will come when men will see that liberty is a gift that must be cherished, defended and worked for. Should the Labour Party move in the direction of those fundamental changes in our economic system to which I have referred, they will find me not their critic but their all too willing supporter.
Yours sincerely,
Andrew MacLaren

After the war his former chief, Duncan, proposed that a title should be conferred for the contribution which the armaments factories had made in Staffordshire. MacLaren immediately suggested an award should be awarded to an engineer, Arthur Smout, whom he had brought in to report on the quality of the production at the two factories. He had advised that brushes and rollers on key machines needed replacing and the implementation of that advice proved a decisive turning point. Later Smout became Director-General of Ammunition Supply at the Ministry of Supply and an executive director of ICI.

In the General Election of July 1945, the Labour Party in Burslem and Tunstall adopted, with prodding from party headquarters, a party candidate. Such a move was done in private with no consultation of Labour supporters. It was a piece of 'the most unscrupulous treachery' said MacLaren. There was little local interest in the Election. At one meeting the audience numbered only 30 and at another no one came at all except for MacLaren and a friend. 'Do not despair at that,' MacLaren advised his friend, 'the immediate task is to write up the report of a mass meeting and send it to the local Press.' The electorate were war-wearied and wanted to hear about Messrs. Beveridge and Attlee's plans for the advent of their 'caring' state.

MacLaren's thoughts on parliamentary party thinking were more incisive at this time than they had been hitherto. 'They [Members of Parliament] must remain mute, even if their consciences prompt them to say something. But the very essence of the British Constitution is this – that a constituency shall freely – freely, mark you – elect a representative to Parliament, there to listen to the discussions, and deliberations in the Councils of State and there to make his decisions, in the interests of those who sent him. Groups outside Parliament were more powerful than Parliament itself. These hirelings are gagged from fear of being thrown out. This party business is becoming nothing but a cancerous growth in the body of the British Constitution. I warn you with the solemnity I can command, that this is going to kill freedom in England.' He dismissed the local Labour Party opposed to him as 'this little group of nobodies.' They were led by George Wigg, the 'earwig', as MacLaren called him, from party headquarters.

MacLaren suffered a heavy defeat, polling only 3223 votes and even losing his deposit. 'I stood in Hanley today without losing an inch of my pride, and lost my election deposit. It was a disaster and I deeply thank these few thousand supporters who have followed me into the political wilderness.'

The Election swept Churchill out and replaced him with Attlee. It was a strange Election, reflecting that the British are a strange folk.

MacLaren had set the Potteries alight with idealism and fervour for fundamental reform. The people were inspired with a large vision but war had drawn a dark curtain across that, finally eclipsing political thought. MacLaren had created that intensity by addressing the fundamental problems, as he had learnt in his Scottish youth. Every economic problem in society has a man-made cause and it is the real business of politics to remove these problems. Unemployment, inflation, poverty, the problems of trade and of foreign exchanges will never be solved by widespread mitigation: they will only be made more intractable. MacLaren inspired the radical element in the Labour Party. They were always a minority and were outnumbered by Socialists with fanciful ideas.

MacLaren might have been more flexible and then won the

Election in 1945. But he would have lived a compromised life and died a corrupted soul with no message to posterity. Weaker men imagine that when they meet with lack of success there must be something wrong in their thinking or their manner. But men of stronger hue see that weakness is not in them, but in the thinking of society at large.

14

Retirement

After his departure from the House of Commons in 1945 MacLaren was inspired immediately to resume teaching political thought. The cause of the blindness in parliament was due to the blindness of the electorate.

He had long given lectures to constituents, foreigners and students. MacLaren had been a founder in 1937 of the School of Economic Science in London with the purpose of teaching fundamental principles about economics and political thought without political bias. The school maintained a branch in Stoke-on-Trent until the early 1950s. The institution later moved from economics to philosophy, first with special regard to Ouspensky and Gurdjieff and later to Plato and Indian spiritual teaching, although MacLaren was not involved with this development.

In 1945 MacLaren was elected an honorary member of the Beefsteak Club. At the time of his election there were only three other honorary members. His membership provided him with friendship and much enjoyment in his later years. The Club was indebted to his insistence to buy the freehold.

He was often struck by the scholarly manner of Hugh Smith who lunched at the club regularly. In conversation he divulged deep knowledge in many subjects. When Smith became deaf, however, his speech often became deafening. One day he declared, in a penetrating voice, that not many members of the club understood the law of rent which outlawed the private ownership of land. MacLaren was astonished at this example of his learning. Later he was surprised to learn, from his published will, that his family had owned Hay's Wharf, which was a land speculator's prime site.

At the Garrick Club, which he joined in the 1960s, MacLaren enlisted the ardent support of the actor Kenneth More. Like someone who has discovered the land question for the first time, More laid into everyone with great enthusiasm. Once he was particularly forceful in a discussion with a collection of actors citing MacLaren as his inspiration, much to MacLaren's embarrassment. After a lifetime of arguing the case, MacLaren had learnt, sometimes, to moderate his zeal. He suggested that More should have more regard for the digestion of his friends than for the land question. 'Ah,' said the actor, 'sometimes you have to thump it home.'

After one heated lunch, MacLaren drove home in a taxi with Sir Malcolm Sargeant. Allowing the embers of the contention to settle they sat in silence, the atmosphere thick with unease. MacLaren had often been called the 'amiable fanatic', but he could be quite uncompromising when opposed in debate about principles of political thought. With good heartiness Sir Malcolm said: 'Andy, we all love you.' Instantly MacLaren stiffened and replied: 'Say that again, and I will call a policeman.'

MacLaren was encouraged by his son to train as a barrister. He found his studies on Roman Law too archaic and laborious to hold his attention long. Nevertheless he fulfilled his obligation to eat the required dinners at Middle Temple. When he fell into conversation with his fellow students, he discovered that they understood as much about natural law as he knew of man-made law, and that their acquaintance with politics was conservative and often reactionary. Natural law could be written, as he put it, on the back of a tram ticket, whereas man's law could only be devised by perusal in books as thick as this, indicating the width by his ample reach. He was no more at home in a wig or gowns than he might have been in military uniform.

MacLaren was happiest painting. In his studio he experimented with the techniques employed by Rembrandt to preserve dark browns from becoming black with age. The secret lay in the manufacture of colours and he was continually experimenting with the technique. He made copies of Rembrandt and Velasquez and painted many original pictures. He was also interested in preserving the colours of old frescoes.

He felt that young artists should learn basic skills and discipline before seriously committing themselves to creative work. Once, in the early 1970s, when looking around a studio in Kensington, with a view to buying it as his home, he was horrified at the state of things before him. The studio was littered with paint, brushes and canvasses covered with abstract designs. When the artist returned from upstairs MacLaren enquired loudly, with a rasping contempt, whether he was in the artist's kitchen?

He had an eye to Nature and an ear for music. One summer evening, he remarked on the gradation of the sky's colour, from a rich blue overhead to a near white on the horizon. 'It is like a water colour with no seam in the whole canvas.' He also found great joy in listening to music, particularly that of Mozart and Hadyn, on the radio.

He was always keen to awaken the artistic sensibilities of people who had been either too lazy or too timid to try their hand. Before and during the Second World War he visited the National Gallery regularly to copy Rembrandt and others. He attracted a small group and would explain to them about the masters' ways of working and their techniques. He became particularly fond of a young German called Karl and treasured his copy of *Tobias and the Angel* by Verrochio. Karl wrote after he had returned home of his horror of war and of his determination to resist becoming involved. Finally, however, he joined up more in fear of the consequences of not doing so. When the correspondence lapsed MacLaren presumed him dead. But Karl had survived the war. In the 1950s his letter arrived to describe his young family and gratitude to MacLaren for those sessions at the Gallery.

MacLaren was asked by Phillip Hendy, the Curator of the National Gallery, in June 1948 to examine Leonardo's *Madonna on the Rocks* which was in need of restoration. MacLaren wrote his opinion in free and elegant script, which itself was a work of beauty.

The canvas already shows small patches where the gesso or paint has broken away; the largest patch showing near the right-hand side on the rock canopy. Closely examined this patch showed signs of previous treatment of restorers. Around its edges were marks of piercings which might have been made around a blister on the surface; through these small holes or piercings the restorer would inject an adhesive substance, then endeavour to press back the blistered paint on to the gesso ground. It is evident that the blistered paint had become brittle and in being pressed the paint cracked and fell away from the surface. The preliminary examination and partial cleaning has brought to the surface the parts previously restored. Considering the age of the picture, and the danger that has threatened its existence, it is in a good state of preservation.

Small sections have been cleared of the old varnish exposing the original painted surface; a section of the cheek of the attending angel, most of the figure of St. John and the right foot of the Infant Christ. The flesh is of cold white in the full lights; the half cast shadows have a beautiful faint purple quality, passing into a deeper warm purples in the full-cast shadow.

I am of the opinion that the entire gesso was covered with a thin coat of dark purply brown allowing the drawing on the gesso to show through. The first painting was them completed in gradations of pure white tempera; from stiff white in the full lights down to mere white glazing in the shadows. The under purply colour painted over by gradations of white gives to the half-cast shadows of the flesh a beautiful dignified warm quality. Having completed this stage of the work the panel would be laid aside to thoroughly dry out and also to allow the glazings in the shadows to "settle". This last detail would be necessary, for in the process of complete drying, the glazings tend to change in tone value – Should changes occur these can be easily remedied, especially where tempera has been used. The first, or under-painting, has been carried forward with consummate skill, and a tenderness, which is characteristic of Leonardo's drawing and painting, pervades those parts of the panel which had been cleared of old superimposed varnish.

Almost in the centre of the picture there are patches of

damaged badly burned surface; these may have been caused by intense heat of candles burning close to the picture. Fortunately this damage is in a full shadow passage of the painting and, if carefully cleaned and partly restored in strict conformity of the painting observed throughout, should not mar the quality of the entire work.

The hands of the Madonna will give rise to a major problem in this restoration. It is doubtful if the artist completed the painting of the hands. The right hand has been painted in by a restorer. The medium used has been oil with the result that there is a darkening in the white which throws the tone quality of the entire hand out of harmony with the original flesh painting of the other parts of the picture. I am inclined to think that the left hand has been scantily and very badly roughed in by a restorer, with utter disregard to the original outline drawing which must have been clearly delineated on the gesso.

Cutting across the infant St. John is a golden cross: this has been superimposed on the original. This 'golden cross' would seem to be a piece of canvas cut to shape, glued to the surface then heavily gilded. It is doubtful whether this piece of canvas can be removed without damaging the canvas.

Andrew MacLaren.

[He added this note]:

When the old coats of varnish have been removed, the flesh painting will appear almost too high in tone. As already noted, the high lights of the flesh painting are pure cold white. In contrast with the sombre colours of the background, this will cause the figures to appear prominent and cold. Originally the flesh painting must have been completed with glazes giving warmth to the flesh and endowing the figures with tonal harmony.

It is clear on examining the cleaning so far completed that these glazings have long since perished. This fact should be noted.

In the late 1950s he was knocked down by a car and lost the keenness of sight which he required for painting. For several years thereafter he seemed to lose his way and life became dull for him.

MacLaren never gave up the dream of a just society. He could not see justice arising from the level of thought which was conveyed to him by the confused output of radio and the newspapers, which for the most part substituted information for thought. Politics had become a cockpit of manoeuvres without grand principles disputing about banalities with a self-interested vigilance; alive not to the welfare of mankind but only to the interests of parties. Indeed it had become a squalid brokerage of votes and State handouts.

MacLaren had a distrust of politicians and he was never deluded by the popular acclaim which was poured on them. He trusted the reasonable man and most certainly not the learned man. He remembered an old Catholic priest once saying after listening to a dispute: 'The more I listen to that fellow, the more I think that if his premises are the smallpox, his deductions will catch the contagion.'

Indeed it must have been a nightmare for him. For the deeper the insight, the more vigilant the observation, the keener must have been the sense of tragedy. Abject physical poverty had been mitigated, at least in its most physical aspects, but MacLaren drew attention to the enormous price. It had dulled political perceptions and it had relocated poverty in minds and in thought; emotions had been trivialised and subjective opinion had supplanted the objectivity of principle. Democracy did not mean that each man's opinion was of equal significance or that society was beholden to the lowest and most general view. It meant that men could govern the society in which they lived according to the best thinking in their midst.

As a Member of Parliament he had always been a realist even though he had seen hopes dashed and much personal tragedy. He was not deceived or even disillusioned by the barbarity of men. If a soul like the Christ could be put to death or a genius like Mozart be flung into a pauper's grave, he was ever alive to both the good and the bad in men.

Despite great faith and courage, MacLaren was reduced to a low state in his 70s. He had seen the complete collapse of that public enthusiasm which had drawn him into public debate during the first decade of the century. When his own powers were dimmed, he became frustrated by his inability to alter that course of events. It amazed him often that men and women seemed to possess little firmness, vision or courage in their political ideas. Ideas seemed to perish as if they were overrun by the tide of fashion.

His son, relying on MacLaren's capacity for teaching, provided him with an opportunity to lecture to about twenty people on Saturday mornings. Leon had a feel for what might be useful to someone struck by misfortune and his kindness and advice to people in that condition was often displayed.

MacLaren had often filled one of the five town halls of the Potteries and attracted as many to the streets outside. But he thought crowd emotion was delusive, substituting cheering for serious thought. It offended MacLaren, as it offended Hamlet. A small class suited him perfectly.

MacLaren revived: his physical and mental demeanour was transformed. His idealism and passion were rekindled and the last years of his life were full and happy.

In the early 1970s, MacLaren went to see a Shakespeare play at the Aldwych theatre. As he sat down he requested a nose clip and a pair of garden shears as he could not see over the large buffon hairstyle of the lady sitting in front of him. Her male companion gallantly changed seats with her, but, as MacLaren had done the same thing with his companion, nothing was resolved, and the protests became more insistent. The woman now became aware that her patience in a hair salon had become the centre of a quarrel and not the focus of admiration. At that point the lights dimmed and there was some delay to the start of the play. In a normal tone, which attracted instant hisses for silence, MacLaren recounted how he had gone from theatre to theatre with Bernard Shaw, who generally reviewed three or more plays a night. If a play contained too many pregnant silences, Shaw used to interject his own lines from his seat. Eventually, MacLaren fell silent, and the play got underway, with the appearance of the chorus. 'Who's he?' demanded MacLaren. On being told that the actor was intended to portray a monk. 'A monk!' exclaimed MacLaren amid further, more irritated, hissing. 'It's an actor dressed in a bed sheet.'

By now his companion felt that he was holding an unpinned hand grenade at a funeral service. There was no chance of escape. He tried to concentrate on a friend's poem; 'This will pass, and this too will pass, and this and this will pass. . . .' But all the time his apprehension was stronger than could be repressed. After two scenes of silence from MacLaren, the queen made her entry nervously. 'Who is she?' MacLaren enquired. 'Bernard always said the English could not act Shakespeare. He preferred the Irish.' At this the audience around him were becoming intensely irritated, and somehow, MacLaren and his companion were forced to make an escape. In the street outside, MacLaren apologised to his companion for spoiling the evening.

On another occasion, at a dinner in a small restaurant, he was seated next to an odd couple. The woman, of about fifty, was expensively dressed and rather bored with her middle-aged companion who was reviewing her investment portfolio. Her only interest was in the number of noughts which expressed her total worth and she evidently thought the details of companies excessively tedious. Every bit of paper was meaningless to her but each told a story which this man was determined to tell. Rolls Royce, for example, still made the finest jet engine in the world but needed time to recover from the blandishments heaped upon them by Mr. Wedgwood-Benn. MacLaren had to be distracted by unbroken conversation. After almost an hour or so, there was a lull in both conservations, and MacLaren reached over to their table, to lay hold of an empty champagne bottle. 'Do you know what I would do with an empty bottle, son?' he enquired loudly of his dining companion, so that the question was addressed rhetorically to everyone. When he was sure he had caught the attention of the room he answered his question 'I would crack it over that woman's head.' She left without further ado and the other diners glowed with appreciation.

Once he intervened fearlessly in a darkening altercation between a cockney milkman and a rich Pakistani. He was visiting a friend for lunch and most would have passed such a commonplace drama prudently. But the street was narrow, and it was impossible to ignore it. Blows were about to be exchanged. MacLaren stepped between the two men. He was a frail looking man with his black hat and bow tie, but the voice was as powerful as their muscles. He admonished the milkman for showing such contemptible racial prejudice and asked the Pakistani to behave better away from home. Both men, who had been incandescent with rage a moment before, were frozen into immobility. As he entered his friend's house, the milkman gathered up a crate of broken bottles and the Pakistani had a fierce argument with his wife in their car.

Travelling home by the Underground MacLaren, then well into his nineties, felt a pickpocket's hand fiddling at his breast pocket. He squeezed it, and squeezed so firmly, that, as he remarked, the owner would never play the piano again. That, he felt, was more memorable and effective than a visit to a magistrates' court and all the scrupulous legality that is extended to suspects caught red-handed.

He visited the city of London in his nineties and near Lloyds insurance market he knocked contemptuously, with his umbrella, on several brass plates displaying names of insurance companies, particularly of life insurance offices. In a street full of milling underwriters MacLaren demanded: 'In the name of God, what is the use of life insurance, if men are dying on their feet?'

He was sometimes asked to speak at meetings of economic students. In a lecture at a college in East London he had argued with academic economists. At length, the resident professor of economics rose to ask him about the cause of unemployment. Before replying MacLaren spotted a fish tank at the back of the room. He asked his audience to imagine what would happen if the tank was emptied of half its water. Would not the natural balance between the fish be disturbed and would not they fight each other? As fish needed water, did not man need . . .? The students murmured in unison 'land'.

He was blessed with good health which he looked after with the aid of herbs. But in his late eighties he was ordered to Brompton Hospital by his doctor. He had difficulty swallowing. He was loathe to consult doctors, preferring natural remedies and after a day he discharged himself.

Health of both mind and emotions was important to him. He felt that many illnesses derived from poor diet and poor housing as well as mental and emotional weakness. A mind possessed of firm ideas was as essential to health, he believed, as a stomach full of nourishment.

Often he dined at a Chinese restaurant called *Yum Sing*, founded by Holland Kwok, whom MacLaren had met when he had arrived as a refugee from Hong Kong. He was then working as a waiter but MacLaren was struck by his evident ability, open character and astute business sense. Today, he directs the *Good Earth* restaurants in and around London.

MacLaren began his meal with prawn crackers, which he called missionaries' toenails, because he was amused how the Church of England had presumed to convert the heirs to one of the wisest and most venerable traditions, the Chinese, to the relatively novel Anglican dogma.

MacLaren often spoke with delight of an occasion, when he attended St. James's Independent School, founded by his son in London. He had been asked to address a group of children on the land question. He had an artist's eye for their beauty but he was drawn as much by the plasticity of their minds.

He loved children. 'The greatest work of art is the child, a human being', he once told Parliament. 'It always startles me that people become apprehensive lest a picture or a chair should be destroyed, yet they pass mankind in the streets, underfed and miserable, and it does not disturb them in the least.'[1]

He found his fulfilment in teaching others. When men finally secure a just, democratic and prosperous society, he may be considered among the very few of its founders. He retained a keen mind and a lively humour, which were always refreshing. He died in April 1975 after a brief illness which affected him only a few days. As he was once observed in the House of Commons, 'The grave-digger, when he is putting MacLaren in his grave, will say, 'There goes land values.'[2]

But the memory of MacLaren will shine brightly in the hearts of those in search of economic justice. One day millions will tread the path that MacLaren trod. The sadness of MacLaren's life was that as the glorious standard unfurled in 1906 by the Prime Minister was overturned, humanity and justice departed

---

[1] Hansard, col. 1170, 26:5:44.
[2] Ibid., col. 514, 23:6:44.

from political economy. However, MacLaren was himself an example of integrity and courage rarely encountered in public life. He detested the designation 'politician'. It did not explain his role. He was a political thinker who linked economic cause and effect.

15

Conclusion

Although MacLaren ventured, somewhat reluctantly, into active politics, he remained unshakeably anchored in principles of political thought. He was interested in clear, cool thinking, regarding party politics as a pantomime of melodrama with scenes, rarely of comedy, often of boredom, tragedy and farce. He did not imagine that enlightenment would suddenly engulf government and the State. The only hope for the real evolution of society lay in the thinking of its people.

Britain has a remarkable history of peaceful, democratic attainment. It has achieved government by the people. It has determined that government shall be as the people will. In civil rights it has achieved a great deal, probably more than any leading nation in recorded history. The civil rights of the monarch and prime minister are the same as the rights of the individual of every rank. Yet, this is but half of what a vision of a free man demands. An individual should be free to earn his living and protect his private property from the rapacious ravages of taxation, he should live in a free, prosperous community, which offers a wide variety of methods of earning a living, he should trade freely with anyone in the world, save a declared enemy, in an economy free of manipulation of exchange and interest rates. None of these rights is recognised in Britain. The individual is oppressed by the Treasury which devise intricate systems of robbing his production and wealth, he is governed by mediocrity and extensive bureaucracy and he lives in a society bedevilled by unemployment, inflation and poverty. Such a society offers a limited range of opportunities to earn a living. The economic picture of society is indeed poor.

CONCLUSION

MacLaren pointed to the spiritual poverty of man. He permits architects, often no more than the lackies of greedy landlords, to plan outrages which spoil the towns and countryside of the 'sceptred isle'. He permits the natural environment to be desecrated. The arts are encouraged to shock with their impudence, perversions and degenerate egoisms.

Most shameful, MacLaren believed, was society's tolerance of economic diseases of poverty. Economic diseases had a cause – the private collection of land value created by the community as a natural fund for public revenue. To lavish government expenditure on welfare, whilst allowing the causes of poverty to persist was sheer hypocrisy and sentimentality. Worse it is stupidity raised on stilts, as MacLaren often referred to it. For the increase in taxation required by a large welfare programme actually exacerbates the condition of poverty which it is intended to relieve. Furthermore, it leaves society in the grip of the vested interests, and politicians who imagine themselves as a hierarchy of potentates. Strip away all the cant and cheap sentimentality and society in Britain is indeed unjust and cruel; an amalgam of self-interest and ignorance. Indeed, Britain finds herself sunk in prejudice and injustice. Unemployment and poverty are raging like cholera and the people are not minded to find the cause of these diseases.

Events in Eastern Europe during the autumn of 1989 show how even the most tyrannical regimes can be brushed aside by the people. Rousseau was right to insist that the people retain the inalienable sovereignty of their society. They cannot delegate this sovereignty to monarchs, to parliaments, to politicians and still less to bureaucrats. All these are the apparatus of public service. The people should know the underlying principles of government and lead their representatives along the path of individual liberty. If the people fall over themselves to watch sports, indulge in mindless pastimes, the acquisition of private gain of monetary wealth and phoney intellectual expertise, and ignore political thought as wantonly as they do in Britain, then they deserve to be dazzled and overwhelmed with the pantomime of Westminster. Until the people develop a *culture* of political thought, they deserve nothing better than the economic slavery which rules at present.

In Britain it is significant that society has no accepted definition of private property. MacLaren defined it as the production of human labour. It is simple to agree with that, but few men have had both the courage and integrity to follow where reason leads to fulfil such a simple truth.

The reform of the fiscal system most dear to Andrew MacLaren has been attempted on three occasions in modern history. Each time it has failed. There will be no fourth time until the people aspire to justice and liberty and leave behind the political docility which they have shown throughout the greater part of the twentieth century. Until they determine the political agenda and return to basic principles, the pantomime of politics will continue and economic problems will remain unresolved. Booms will give way to recession in a perpetual cycle; the landowner will cream off the gains of the boom and the landless will suffer the intensification of poverty during recessions.

A fitting memorial to the stand made by MacLaren, Churchill, George, Turgot and others of like mind, would be the removal of politics from political thought, in the same way it has been removed from arithmetic.

Perhaps the essence of Andrew MacLaren's political thought was this profound utterance in the House of Commons:

Whether it be in politics, philosophy, religion or anything else, the one cardinal characteristic of truth is simplicity. The greatest truth that man ever heard was spoken [by Christ] in the language of simplicity in the streets of Jerusalem. Simplicity and truth stand together, and whenever you get into complexity, beware, because there is a falsity in it somewhere.[1]

---

[1] Hansard, col. 2098, 24:2:37.

Index

Amalgamated Society of Engineers, 46, 163.
Asquith, Herbert, 30, pensions 1908, 31, value of land, 31–2, 44, 62, MacLaren & Asquith, 82.
Astor, Viscountess, 79.

Baldwin, Stanley, 74, 95–6, 151, Curzon's view of, 82, calls Election 1923, 85, visits Stoke, 91–3, becomes PM, 153.
Balfour, Arthur, 27, 28.
Basingstoke, war service, 46–8.
BBC, 160, 168–9.
Beefsteak Club, 175–6.
Beaverbrook, Lord, 79, 128.
Belloc, Hilaire, 32.
Bevin, Aneurin, 142, 168.
Beveridge, Sir William, 164–7.
Boer War, 27–8.
Bonar-Law, Andrew, 30, 82.
Bryce, James 17.
Buckle, Henry, 60.
Burke, Edmond, 50, 69.
Burslem, Labour candidate, 60–2, Member of Parliament, 64, *Labour Chronicle*, 86.

Cadogan, Edward, 139.

Campbell-Bannerman, Sir Henry, 28–30, 121, opposed by Lords, 29, death of wife, 30, death of, 32.
Caricature, first experience 3, Glasgow School of Art, 4, in Parliament, 73–6.
Cause of economic ills, 80, 153–4
Cavor, Camillo, 121.
Cecil, Lord David, 66, 72.
Chamberlain, Austen, 1909 Budget, 38, coalition, 63.
Chamberlain, Joe, 3, 28.
Chamberlain, Neville, 79, 149, Munich '38, 159–60, portrait of, 160–7, is deserted, 161.
Charing Cross Bridge project, 134.
Chesterton, G. K., 147.
Christ, Jesus, 90, 188.
Churchill, Winston, 17, 18, 30, 35, *The Peoples Rights*, 34, Chancellor, 79, joins protectionism, 83, practices protectionism, 122–4, his former philosophy, 131, describes MacDonald, 135, MacLaren describes, 144, becomes PM, 161.
Clutton-Brock, Arthur, 65.
Cobden, Richard, 121–2, 190.
Credit Anstalt Bank collapse of, 141.

Curzon, Marquis, 82.

Dawes Plan, 85.
Duncan, Sir Ian, works for, 163, 172.
Douglas-Home, William, 168.

Eden, Anthony, 159.
Edward V11, 30, 33.
Elgar, Sir Edward, 5.

Fels, Joseph, 21, 39.
Financial crash 1931, beginnings of, 134.
First World War, declared 39, cause of, 40, cost 43, recruitment, 44–5, end of, 49, loss of life, 52, effect on political thinking, 50, financing of, 54.
Football, 94, 127–8.
Foreign Office, 43, 57.
Foster, Lord, 58.

Garrick Club, 175–6.
General Elections, *1906*, 28, *1910*, 36, *1919 [coupon]*, 52, *1922*, 64–5, *1923*, 85, 89, *1924*, 85, 100, *1929*, 96, *1931*, 146–7, *1935*, 153, *1945*, 172–3.
General Strike, 95.
George V, 34, 91.
George, Henry, first reading of 7, his life 8, writes *Progress and Poverty*, 9, visits Britain, 15.
Gracci, 168.
Gregory Committee, 141.
Greenwood, Arthur, 170.

Hardy, Keir, 21.
Heath, Edward, 30
Henderson, Arthur, 93, 144.
Hitler, 159.
Home, Lord, foreword, 31, 167.

House of Commons, Members' remuneration, 70, motivation of Members, 70–1, on politicians, 184–5.
House of Lords, rejection of 1909 Budget, 33, MacLaren's opinion of, 68.

Indian Independence, 55–6.
Independent Labour Party, 153, 175.
Irish Question, 56, 62.

Keynes, John Maynard, 61, brushes aside free trade, 122, 128–9, 133, 141–2, 157, 167.
Kitchener, Lord, 47.
Kwok, Holland, foreword, 184.

Lal, Chaman, 53–4.
Land Song, 36, 48, 64.
Lansbury, George, 54, 56, dispute with Northumberland, 107–11, on protectionism, 128–31, 147, 160.
Lansdowne, Lord, 20–1.
League of Nations, 76.
Lloyd George, David, 28, 30, 74, Budget 1909, 31–4, Limehouse speech, 32–3, land taxes 32, sale of honours, 63, resigned 63, wit of, 71–3, 83, 125, Budget 1931, 136, 137.
Low, David, 75.

MacDonald, Ramsay, 21, 74, 122, 129, 132, forms Union of Democratic Control, 40, 'Ma dear friends', 78, PM, 85, McVitie case, 87, Campbell Case, 87, Zinovieff letter, 88, loses 1924 election, 88, coalition government of, 143–153, described by AJP

INDEX

Taylor, 145, attacked by MacLaren, 151, resigns, 153, death of 161.

MacLaren, Andrew, grandmother, 1, family 2, school 3, drawing 3, monks 4, engineering, 4, Glasgow School of Art 5, politics in Glasgow 7, an Englishman, 43–4, pacificism 47, war service, 48–51, adopted as candidate at Wimbledon, 53, at Burslem, 60, returned as MP 64, maiden speech 66–7, parliamentary wit, 82, values Parliament, 67–8, loses Election of *1923*, 85, *Labour Chronicle*, 86, exposes local council, 88–9, friendship with Baldwin, 91–3, speaks of art, 97–8, warns about protectionism, 129–30, Charing Cross Bridge, 134, quotes L G in 1931, 138, defines property, 139–40, leaves House with Snowden 1931, 142, attacks government, 146, 151, introduces Private Bill, 156–7, praises Chamberlain, 160, leads him from Commons, 161, war service 163–4, warns about reconstruction, 164, attacks bureaucracy, 169, health of, 183, talk to children, 184, death of, 184, on simplicity and truth, 188, Writings,
  Genesis of War, 41–2,
  Cleaning *Virgin on the Rocks*, 177–9.

MacLaren, John, son, 55.
MacLaren Leon, son, 175, 181.
Macpherson, Ian, 47, 49.

Macmillan Committee, 132, 142.
Mcnabb, Vincent, 147.
Marjoribanks, Andrew, 139–40.
Marshall, Alfred, 16.
Masterman, Charles, 40, 86.
May Committee, 135, 143.
Marx, Karl, 5, 6, 19.
Maxton, Jimmy, 19–20, 74, 155, 160.
Middle Temple, 176.
Mill, John Stuart, 25.
Monarchy, 68, 155.
Monastery, 3–4.
Montrose, Duke of, 20.
More, Kenneth, 175.
Morrison, Herbert, 157.
Mosley, Sir Oswald, 95, 128–9, 154–5.
Mosley, Cynthia, 128.

National Gallery, 177–9.
National Government, formation of, 147, MacLaren's view of, 151, 161.
Northumberland, Duke of, dispute with, 99–107.
Nulty, Bishop, 14.

Parliament Act 1911, 35–6.
Protectionism, 13, 63, of British films, 125, returns in 1931, 150–3.

O'Connor, T.P., 68.

Religion, 90, 94–5, 123.
Russia, 162.

Shaw, Bernard., 15, 78, 110, correspondence with, 107–120.
Sargent, Sir Malcolm, xi, 176.
Second World War, MacLaren warns of in 1922, 62,

MacLaren attacks state bureaucracy, 175.
Smith, Hugh, 176.
Snowden, Philip, 43, 95, 130, first Budget 1924, 85, 88, inheritance in 1929, 132–3, sets up Macmillan Committee, 132, Budget of 1931, 135–6, attacks landlordism, 133–4, on land taxes, 135–6, leaves House with MacLaren, 142, attacks Labour Party, 147, resigns, 151, emergency Budget of 1931, 145, on villainy of MacDonald, 152, dies 155.
Socialists, 70.
Spencer, Herbert, 11–2, 41.
St Joseph's Church, 97–8.
Stoke-on-Trent, area of, 63, MacLaren's view of, 81, Priestley's view of, 81, MacLaren exposes Council, 93.
Suffrage, 52.

Tavistock, Marquis of, 147.
Taxation, 80, 158.
Thomas, Jimmy, 128, 149, expelled from Commons, 155, 169–70.
Tolstoy, Leo, 16–7.
Trevelyan, Charles, 52, 53.
Tullibardine, Marquis of, 25.

Unemployment, in 1921, 90, in 1930, 137, 146, 149.
Union of Democratic Control, 40, 42.
United Committee for the Taxation of Land Values, 43, 83, 91, 152.

Wall Street crash, 132.
Washinmgton Conference, 60.
Wedgwood, J, 47, 52, 77, 157.
Wheatley, John , 88.
White, Dundas, 52, 61–2, 77.
Wimbdelon, 57–8, lectures in, 60–1, local election 58.
Women, speeches to, 58, 62, 84, 162.